ASEAN ENVIRONMENTAL LI INTEGRATION

While the environmental performance of most Association of Southeast Asian Nations (ASEAN) member states is above the world average, ASEAN nations will continue to face growing environmental challenges due to pressures exerted on them such as population growth, urbanization and industrialization. The authors of this book look at how the member states of ASEAN employ law as a means of regional integration within the context of environmental conservation. While the goal of new laws is to implement sustainable development, it continues to be an ongoing adaptive process, since clear and immediate answers to environmental challenges are rarely available. Readers of this book will gain a clear idea of the evolving cooperation for sustainability within ASEAN at regional and global levels, and the areas of focus for the future. The book will be of interest to policy and decision-makers, as well as environmental organizations and academics in the field.

Koh Kheng-Lian is Emeritus Professor at the Faculty of Law at the National University of Singapore, and former Director of the Asia-Pacific Centre for Environmental Law (APCEL). She was IUCN-Commission for Environmental Law Regional Vice-Chair for South and East Asia, and a member of its Steering Committee.

Nicholas A. Robinson is Gilbert and Sarah Kerlin Distinguished Professor Emeritus at Pace Law School, USA, and also serves as Adjunct Professor at the Yale School of Forestry & Environmental Studies. He was chair of the IUCN-Commission for Environmental Law, and Legal Advisor to IUCN.

Lye Lin-Heng is Director of the Asia-Pacifi c Centre for Environmental Law (APCEL) and former Vice-Dean of the Faculty of Law, National University of Singapore (NUS). She is Visiting Associate Professor at the Yale School of Forestry & Environmental Studies and former Vice- Chair of the IUCN Academy of Environmental Law and a member of its Board of Governors, representing South-east Asia.

INTEGRATION THROUGH LAW

The Role of Law and the Rule of Law in ASEAN Integration

General Editors
J. H. H. Weiler, European University Institute
Tan Hsien-Li, National University of Singapore

The Association of Southeast Asian Nations (ASEAN), comprising the ten member states of Brunei Darussalam, Cambodia, Indonesia, Lao PDR, Malaysia, Myanmar, Philippines, Singapore, Thailand and Vietnam, has undertaken intensified integration into the ASEAN Community through the Rule of Law and Institutions in its 2007 Charter. This innovative book series evaluates the community-building processes of ASEAN to date and offers a conceptual and policy toolkit for broader Asian thinking and planning of different legal and institutional models of economic and political regional integration in the region. Participating scholars have been divided up into six separate thematic strands. The books combine a mix of Asian and Western scholars.

Centre for International Law, National University of Singapore (CIL-NUS)

The Centre for International Law (CIL) was established in 2009 at the National University of Singapore's Bukit Timah Campus in response to the growing need for international law expertise and capacity building in the Asia-Pacific region. CIL is a university-wide research centre that focuses on multidisciplinary research and works with other NUS or external centres of research and academic excellence. In particular, CIL collaborates very closely with the NUS Faculty of Law.

INTEGRATION THROUGH LAW
The Role of Law and the Rule of Law in ASEAN Integration
General Editors: J. H. H. Weiler and Tan Hsien-Li

ASEAN ENVIRONMENTAL LEGAL INTEGRATION

Sustainable Goals?

KOH KHENG-LIAN,
NICHOLAS A. ROBINSON
AND LYE LIN-HENG

CAMBRIDGE
UNIVERSITY PRESS

CAMBRIDGE
UNIVERSITY PRESS

University Printing House, Cambridge CB2 8BS, United Kingdom

Cambridge University Press is part of the University of Cambridge.

It furthers the University's mission by disseminating knowledge in the pursuit of education, learning and research at the highest international levels of excellence.

www.cambridge.org
Information on this title: www.cambridge.org/9781316604311

First published 2016

A catalogue record for this publication is available from the British Library

ISBN 978-1-316-60431-1 Paperback

CONTENTS

TABLES

GENERAL EDITORS' PREFACE

This monograph is published within the context of a wide-ranging research project entitled Integration Through Law: The Role of Law and the Rule of Law in ASEAN Integration (ITL), undertaken by the Centre for International Law at the National University of Singapore and directed by J. H. H. Weiler and Tan Hsien-Li.

The Preamble to the ASEAN Charter concludes with a single decision: "We, the Peoples of the Member States of the Association of Southeast Asian Nations … [h]ereby decide to establish, through this Charter, the legal and institutional framework for ASEAN." For the first time in its history of over four decades, the Legal and the Institutional were brought to the forefront of ASEAN discourse.

The gravitas of the medium, a Charter: the substantive ambition of its content, the creation of three interlocking Communities, and the turn to law and institutions as instruments for realization provide ample justification for this wide-ranging project, to which this monograph is one contribution, examining ASEAN in a comparative context.

That same substantive and, indeed, political ambition means that any single study, illuminating as it may be, will cover but a fraction of the phenomena. Our modus operandi in this project was to create teams of researchers from Asia and elsewhere who would contribute individual monographs within an overall framework which we had designed.

The project framework, involving several thematic clusters within each monograph, is thus determined by the framework and the place of each monograph within it.

As regards the specific content, however, the authors were free, indeed encouraged, to define their own understanding of the problem and their own methodology and reach their own conclusions. The thematic structure of the entire project may be found at the end of this Preface.

The project as a whole, and each monograph within it, display several methodological sensibilities.

First, law, in our view, can only be understood and evaluated when situated in its political and economic context. Thus, the first studies in the overall project design are intended to provide the political, economic, cultural and historical context against which one must understand ASEAN and are written by specialists in these respective disciplines. This context, to a greater or lesser degree, also informs the sensibility of each monograph. There are no "black letter law" studies to be found in this project and, indeed, even in the most technical of areas we encouraged our authors to make their writing accessible to readers of diverse disciplines.

Comparative experience suggests that the success of achieving some of the more ambitious objectives outlined in Article 1 of the Charter will depend in no small measure on the effectiveness of legal principles, legal rules and legal institutions. This is particularly true as regards the success of establishing "an ASEAN Community comprising the ASEAN Security Community, the ASEAN Economic Community and the ASEAN Socio-Cultural Community as provided for in the Bali Declaration of

ASEAN Concord II". Article 2(2)(n) stipulates the commitment of ASEAN member states to act in accordance with the principle of "adherence to multilateral trade rules and ASEAN's rules-based regimes for effective implementation of economic commitments and progressive reduction towards elimination of all barriers to regional economic integration." The ASEAN member states therefore envisage that rules of law and the Rule of Law will become a major feature in the future of ASEAN. Although, as seen, the Charter understands itself as providing an institutional and legal framework for ASEAN, the question of the "role of law and the rule of law" is not advocacy but a genuine enquiry in the various substantive areas of the project as to:

- the substantive legal principles and substantive rules of the various ASEAN communities;
- the procedural legal principles and rules governing institutional structures and decision-making processes;
- implementation, enforcement and dispute settlement.

One should not expect a mechanical application of this scheme in each study; rather, a sensibility that refuses to content itself with legal enactments as such and looks to a "living" notion of law and institutions is ubiquitous in all the studies. Likewise, the project is sensitive to "non Law." It variously attempts to locate the appropriate province of the law in this experience. That is, not only the role of law, but also the areas that are and should remain outside the reach of legal institutionalization with due sensitivity to ASEAN and Asian particularism and political and cultural identities.

The project, and the monographs of which it is made, are not normatively thick. They do not advocate. They are designed, for the most part, to offer reflection, discuss the pros and cons, and in this way enrich public awareness, deepen understanding of different options and in that respect contribute indirectly to policymaking.

This decisive development of ASEAN has been accompanied by a growing Asian interest in various legal and institutional forms of transnational economic and political cooperation, notably the various voices discussing and showing an interest in an East Asia Integration project. The number of Free Trade Agreements (FTAs) and Regional Trade Agreements (RTAs) has increased from six in 1991 to 166 in 2013, with a further 62 in various stages of negotiations.

Methodologically, the project and many of the monographs are comparative in their orientation. Comparative law is one of the few real-life laboratories that we have in which to assess and understand the operation of different legal and institutional models designed to tackle similar objectives and problems. One should not need to put one's own hand in the fire to learn that it scorches. With that in mind a couple of monographs offer both conceptual reflection and pragmatic "tool boxing" on some of the key elements featuring in all regional integration systems.

Comparative law is in part about divergence: it is a potent tool and means to understand one's own uniqueness. One understands better the uniqueness of Apples by comparing them to Oranges. You understand better the specialness of a Toyota by comparing it to a Ford.

Comparative law is also about convergence: it is a potent tool and means to understand how what are seemingly different phenomena are part of a broader trend, an insight which may enhance both self-understanding and policy potentialities.

Although many studies in the project could have almost immediate policy implications, as would the project as a whole, this is not its only or even principal purpose. There is a rich theory of federalism which covers many countries around the world. There is an equally rich theory of European integration, which has been associated with the advent Union. There is also considerable learning on Free Trade Areas and the like.

To date, the study of the legal aspects of ASEAN specifically and other forms of Asian legal integration has been derivative of, and dependent on, theoretical and conceptual insight which were developed in different contexts.

One principal objective of ITL and these monographs will be to put in place the building blocks for an authentic body of ASEAN and Asian integration theory developed in, and with sensitivity to, the particularities and peculiarities of the region and continent. A theory and conceptual framework of Asian legal integration will signal the coming of age of research of and in the region itself.

Although the monographs form part of an overarching project, we asked our authors to write each as a "standalone" – not assuming that their readers would have consulted any of the other titles. Indeed, the project is rich and few will read all monographs. We encourage readers to pick and choose from the various monographs and design their own menu. There is, on occasion, some overlap in providing, for example, background information on ASEAN in different studies. That is not only inevitable but desirable in a project of this amplitude.

The world is increasingly witnessing a phenomenon of interlocking regional organization where the experience of one feeds on the others. In some way, the intellectual, disciplinary and comparative sensibility of this project is a microcosm of the world it describes.

The range of topics covered in this series comprises:

The General Architecture and Aspirations of ASEAN
The Governance and Management of ASEAN: Instruments, Institutions, Monitoring, Compliance and Dispute Resolution
Legal Regimes in ASEAN
The ASEAN Economic Community
ASEAN and the World
The Substantive Law of ASEAN

FOREWORD

It gives me pleasure to write the foreword to this important monograph by three good friends.

Emeritus Professor Koh Kheng-Lian, Emeritus Professor Nicholas A. Robinson and Associate Professor Lye Lin-Heng are three outstanding scholars of environmental law. Both Koh and Robinson have won the Elizabeth Haub Prize for Environmental Law. Koh was former IUCN–WCEL (International Union for Conservation of Nature-World Commission on Environmental Law) Regional Vice-Chair for South and East Asia and a member of its Governing Board, and Robinson was former Chair of IUCN-WCEL and its Governing Board.

Koh initiated a course on ASEAN Environmental Law, Policy and Governance at the Faculty of Law, National University of Singapore (NUS), and has given extensive lectures on the subject in the University of Mexico, the William Richardson School of Law of the University of Hawaii, USA and also a number of law schools in the ASEAN countries.

Robinson and Lye co-teach Comparative Environmental Law at the School of Forestry at Yale University. Lye is the co-founder of the highly successful Master's program on Environmental Management at NUS, and teaches environmental law at NUS, Yale University and the University of Sydney. She is a member of the Board of Governors of the IUCN Academy of Environmental Law.

ASEAN is undergoing a historic transition, from an association to a community by 2015. The adoption of the ASEAN Charter in 2008 was a turning point. ASEAN's ambition is to be a rule-based organization and to take its commitments seriously. It is in this context that the Centre for International Law, NUS and New York University's Law School have jointly launched a major research project on ASEAN integration and the role that law plays in this process.

This monograph is one of a series covering different aspects of ASEAN integration.

I am glad that environment has been included as one book in this series. As the authors have pointed out, over the past thirty-five years, ASEAN has enacted a large corpus of declarations, principles and treaties relating to the environment. My impression is that, in some cases, not all the ASEAN countries have ratified the agreements or implemented other instruments. In other cases, even if all ASEAN countries have ratified an agreement, the implementation has been less than satisfactory. This could be due to a lack of capacity or lack of political will or simply to bad governance. We must develop a culture of taking our commitments seriously.

I thank the authors for their honest evaluation of the progress ASEAN has achieved and for their recommendations on what ASEAN should do in the future. Southeast Asia has one of the world's richest biodiversity. It is also the home of some of the world's largest remaining rain forests. ASEAN countries are rapidly urbanizing. There is therefore much at stake environmentally. Let us hope that the leaders of ASEAN will heed the recommendations of the authors.

Tommy Koh
Chair
Centre for International Law, NUS

ACKNOWLEDGMENTS

The authors are pleased to thank the following individuals for their assistance in the preparation of this study: Our able research assistant, Ms. Audrey Kang, J.D. candidate, Pace University School of Law (Pace); Ms. Lorraine Rubich (Pace); Ms. Taryn Rucinski, Environmental Law Reference Librarian, Pace; Ms. Nicole Chua, Mr. Samuel Loke, and Mr. Peh Zu Hao – LLB students, Law Faculty, National University of Singapore (NUS); Ms. Shirley Mak, Secretary of APCEL, Faculty of Law, NUS; and the following experts who provided the authors with country reports on the state of environmental law and cooperation through ASEAN in their respective nations:

Indonesia – Dr. Laode M Syarif, Hasanuddin University, Makassar-Indonesia

Malaysia – Associate Professor Azmi Sharom, University of Malaya

Myanmar – Mr. James Finch, Ms. Saw Yu Win, and Soe Phone Myint, Myanmar Thanlwin Legal Services Ltd

Philippines – Professor Gloria Ramos, University of Philippines in Cebu

Thailand – Ms. Weerada Tivasuradej, Office of the Administrative Court, Thailand

Vietnam – Mr. Vo Trung Tin, Ho Chi Minh University and Ms. Nguyen Phuc Thuy Hien, PC Vietnam Ltd.

The authors are grateful to Professor Koh Kheng-Lian for compiling and editing extensive sets of documents on the environmental law of ASEAN, and commends ASEAN for providing access to its environmental legal materials and World Scientific for undertaking this publication. See K. -L. Koh, *ASEAN Environmental Law, Policy and Governance: Selected Documents* (volumes I (2009) and II (2012)). These two volumes are indispensible to anyone studying ASEAN environmental law and policy.

The authors assume responsibility for any errors and omissions. This is the first study of its kind involving environmental law across the ASEAN member states, and the authors would be grateful to receive comments or suggestions from readers.

Introduction: exploring environmental law in Southeast Asia

> The environmental performance of most ASEAN Member States, as assessed by reputable studies, is above the world average, and the ecological footprint is much lower than that of many nations. However, ASEAN will continue to face growing environmental challenges given the need to lift a third of its population earning less than $2 a day out of poverty, and the many other pressures exerted on the environment such as population growth, urbanization and industrialization.
>
> Dr. Surin Pitsuwan, ASEAN Secretary-General[1]

Environment is *sans frontières.* Many of the current or emerging environmental problems are transnational and transboundary, necessitating legal integration, whether in the form of hard or soft laws, programs, policies or governance innnovations, such as ASEAN Dialogue Partners, or the United Nations Environment Programme consultations. All these are crucial to ASEAN.[2]

1 S. Pitsuwan, "Foreword" in Fourth ASEAN State of the Environment Report, 2009.

2 Throughout this volume, the law is as stated on April 30, 2015, but some parts were updated while the manuscript was in press. Web

ASEAN is part of the global order for environmental sustainability. It is a partner of the United Nations in the field of development. As the 1971 Stockholm Conference on the Human Environment and the 1992 "Earth Summit" at Rio De Janiero have made clear, we the peoples of the United Nations and of ASEAN alike, share one world, one atmosphere, one stratosphere. ASEAN's economic pillar requires integration to move Southeast Asia forward, and environment must move *in tandem* to prevent degradation of ecosystems for development to be sustainable regionally and globally.

This monograph examines the phenomenon of "integration through law" (ITL), or more particularly how the member states of ASEAN employ law as a means of regional integration, focusing in particular on how this process functions in the context of environmental conservation and sustainable development. The several chapters trace ASEAN's struggles to integrate environment within its own community and also with the global community. There are many concerns, not only in terms of the lack of institutional capacity and funding, but in the very nature of environmental problems. The environmental sciences have taught nations how complicated and interrelated human impacts are on the climate or ecosystems. States are left grappling with solutions. The search for environmentally sustainable progress is an ongoing, adaptive process, often without clear, immediate answers. This complexity is compounded by too many inputs

addresses were correct at the date of submission of the manuscript to the publisher on April 30, 2015.

that national sectors receive from diverse interdisciplinary studies, without any governance system to connect them.

As ASEAN member states seek ways to cooperate on environmental problems, moreover, the sought-for integration must begin with a mindset shared by all ASEAN member states: that regional cooperation must not be an interference with domestic affairs. When ASEAN was established in 1967, regionalism was being developed side by side with nationalism within each of the then founder members, which had just gained independence from their colonial masters. Hence, there was a clinging to the Westphalian principles of sovereignty and non-interference with domestic affairs. Even years later when regional integration was first mooted, it was regarded as a "dirty word" by some ASEAN members, which regarded it as wresting from them their hard-earned sovereignty. Even today, over forty years on, the ASEAN Charter 2007 embodies this principle and that of non-interference, although much debate has modified the concepts and reshaped their calibration.

In 2015, ASEAN is caught on the horns of its own dilemma. It seeks both the benefits of regional trade and environmental sustainability, while jealously protecting national (or sub-national) prerogatives. This is evident when ASEAN introduced the concept of "non-traditional security" in its political-security pillar, which covers transnational crimes and transboundary challenges. The scope of non-traditional security can include illegal trade in endangered species. This inconsistency in approach has, as yet, not been widely recognized. What ASEAN requires today is a robust interpretation of the non-traditional security approach that would facilitate an evolution of the understanding of the traditional ASEAN Way. Some recommendations to foster environmental sustainability within ASEAN are set forth in Chapter 5 of this monograph.

Southeast Asia is one of the richest regions in biodiversity in the world. It includes three mega-diverse countries (Indonesia, Malaysia and the Philippines); five mainland riverine systems within the states of Cambodia, Lao PDR, Myanmar, Thailand and Vietnam; and one-third of the world's coral reefs. It is a pathway for international migration of many species of birds and fish. Its member states have some of the longest coastlines in the world, each facing the problems of rising sea levels. Indonesia has counted some 1,500 islands that are now threatened with submersion by rising sea levels.[3] The environment is of extreme importance to the ten nation states of Southeast Asia that are ASEAN members. Their regional cooperation can enhance environmental adaptation toward a robust socio-economic future. The environmental pillar is essential for sustainable development, as all nations observed in the United Nations 2002 Johannesburg Plan of Implementation. This monograph explores the pathways ASEAN is forging to build its environmental pillar for its members' collective and individual sustainable development.

[3] BBC, "Rising sea 'threatens 1,500 islands,'" February 25, 2014, www.bbc.co.uk/news/blogs-news-from-elsewhere-26337723; Sanskrity Sinha, "Indonesia Losing 1,500 Islands to Rising Sea," *International Business Times*, February 26, 2014, www.ibtimes.co.uk/indonesia-losing-1500-islands-rising-sea-1438000.

ASEAN was first established on August 8, 1967, with the signing of the Bangkok Declaration, "to establish a firm foundation for common action to promote regional cooperation in South-East Asia in the spirit of equality and partnership and thereby contribute towards peace, progress and prosperity in the region." There were then only five parties (Indonesia, Malaysia, Philippines, Thailand and Singapore). The focus then was on "the cherished ideals of peace, freedom, social justice and economic well-being." This was before the 1972 UN Conference on the Human Environment held in Stockholm. The environment was not yet a geo-political or diplomatic concern. Since then ASEAN added to its list of members and now has ten members, with the addition of Brunei (January 7, 1984), Vietnam (July 28, 1995), Lao PDR and Myanmar (July 23, 1997) and Cambodia (November 30, 1999). As ASEAN membership increased, the environment loomed as an even more important rationale for regional cooperation.

When the UN Conference in Stockholm in 1972 agreed on the Stockholm Declaration, it drew the attention of ASEAN to examining the common environmental problems on a regional as well as national level. This focus led to the ASEAN Sub-Regional Environment Programme (ASEP), Phase I (1978–82), which subsequently entered into Phase II (1983–87) and Phase III (1988–92). When in 1992 the UN Conference on Environment and Development (UNCED, or the "Earth Summit") held at Rio de Janeiro adopted the Rio Declaration on Environment and Development and Agenda 21, ASEAN took many steps forward. UNCED compelled each state to take stock of its environment and develop its own green plan to work toward sustainable development in the spirit of Agenda 21 ("Earth's Action Plan"). ASEAN started its ASEAN Strategic Plan of Action on the Environment, 1994–1998. This was followed by the Hanoi Plan of Action, 1999–2004 (Strategy 6 was to Protect the Environment and Promote Sustainable Development); and the Vientiane Action Programme, 2004–2010, which sought to realize an "ASEAN Socio-Cultural Community" and to promote "Environmental Sustainability." These progressive and reiterative measures are building ASEAN's regional environmental cooperation, as this monograph discusses for the first time.

In 2007, all parties agreed to and signed the ASEAN Charter, which provided ASEAN with a much-needed legal personality. This heralded a new chapter in ASEAN's history. It has restructured ASEAN's institutional framework so as to enable ASEAN's Vision 2020 – "One vision, One Identity, One Caring and Sharing Society." ASEAN's Vision 2020 has mechanisms for strengthening compliance in all areas including the environment. The Charter resolves "to ensure sustainable development for the benefit of present and future generations and to place the well-being, livelihood and welfare of the peoples at the centre of the ASEAN community building process." ASEAN's Vision 2020 was succeeded by the ASEAN Socio-Cultural Community Blueprint (ASCC) (2009–2015), as part of the Roadmap for an ASEAN Community from 2009 to 2015. The Roadmap also includes the ASEAN Political-Security Community Blueprint, the ASEAN Economic Community Blueprint and the Initiative for ASEAN Integration Work Plan II (2009–2015). These measures will be examined in this monograph, in the course of addressing the issue of ASEAN's integration through environmental law.

The ASEAN Way as a foundation for regional cooperation involves decision by consensus, non-confrontational resolution of disputes, respect for the principles of sovereignty and non-intervention. This admirable framework for decision-making does pose challenges to resolving environmental problems. Such decision-making takes time, and meanwhile many environmental trends accelerate. There have been many initiatives to address environmental issues at the ASEAN level, including the formal meetings of the Ministers for the Environment, or meetings of senior officials on the environment, or collaboration through specific programs on the environment as mentioned above. ASEAN has also adopted numerous soft-law instruments on the environment, which take the form of Declarations, Resolutions, Statements and Accords, as well as hard-law instruments, notably the ASEAN Agreement on Nature and Natural Resources (1985) and the ASEAN Agreement on Transboundary Haze Pollution (2002). More recently, ASEAN has added a few more hard-law agreements.

The fact is that the environment today has become of great importance to the Member States of ASEAN. Its people have always relied on the environment for their livelihoods, whether directly or indirectly, and will continue to do so. These valuable natural resources and the region's biodiversity are, however, under extreme threat from human activities, as the region pursues rapid economic development. Industrialization has led to considerable and grave air, water, land and noise pollution. Increased urban settlements present problems in housing, health and food security. Illegal logging and unsustainable forest management have led to the depletion of natural resources and loss of wild flora and fauna. The marine and terrestrial wealth of the region is vanishing. Species have been lost or are on the brink of extinction. Indeed the region is a major hotspot for illegal trade in endangered species. Climate change has also brought extreme storms leading to massive floods in recent years. ASEAN nations are caught between national policies that strive to improve their economic well-being but that may have deleterious effects on the environment, and holistic aspirations to view ASEAN as one eco-system.

How has Southeast Asia as a region coped with these challenges? ASEAN works on consensus and cooperation, as well as through capacity-building. The ASEAN Way – involving decision by consensus, non-confrontational resolution of disputes, respect for the principles of sovereignty, and non-intervention – on the whole fosters informality, quiet diplomacy, face-saving, and an aversion to enforceable new legal instruments (i.e. hard law). Worries exist about whether an inability to comply with a treaty might subject a member state to inference in its domestic affairs. This worry, in turn, often masks a reluctance to tackle tough environmental challenges, especially as new regulations might curb patterns of economic gain or disrupt vested interests. Nonetheless, ASEAN has made notable efforts in regional environmental management, particularly in the realm of biodiversity conservation. Some examples include the establishment of the ASEAN Centre for Biodiversity, the designation of some thirty-five ASEAN Heritage Parks[4] across the ten ASEAN member states pursuant to the ASEAN Declaration on Heritage Parks and the establishment of the ASEAN Wildlife Enforcement Network (ASEAN-WEN), which is the largest wildlife law enforcement network in the world. A notable recent achievement is Indonesia's ratification of the 2002 ASEAN Agreement on Transboundary Haze Pollution, the last state to do so. Indonesia's adherence to the 2002 Haze Agreement in 2014 took place soon after Singapore passed its Transboundary Haze Pollution Act (September 2014), which was enacted to address air pollution caused by forest fires in neighboring countries, particularly Indonesia. However, the ASEAN Agreement on Nature and Natural Resources, signed in Kuala Lumpur in 1985, is still not in force, because three member states have yet to ratify (Brunei, Malaysia and Singapore). More recently, ASEAN has been more robust in tackling zoonotic diseases and disaster management compared to its tardy actions in other areas.

This monograph provides the first comprehensive review of ASEAN's attempts at legal integration in its environmental laws. Southeast Asia is experiencing rapid economic growth and a growing population. If it is to continue to provide potable water, healthy air and adequate food, and sustain renewable natural resources, it will need to build environmental stewardship and laws into its development practices. This monograph explores how ASEAN endeavors

[4] As of October 2014 – see http://chm.aseanbiodiversity.org/index.php?option=com_wrapper&view=wrapper&Itemid=110&current=110.

to accomplish these ends. The analysis is provided in six chapters.

Chapter 1 introduces approaches to environmental sustainability in the context of the ASEAN member states, along with a succinct overview of regional collaborative efforts at the ASEAN level. Integration is examined in the context of both institutional integration and integration of laws and policies. Chapter 2 introduces the elements of state practice for sustainability, emphasizing the need for a sound environmental management system, which requires a stable institutional system that is not yet present in some of the ASEAN member states.

Chapter 3 surveys the unique environmental attributes of Southeast Asia. It provides a physical overview of the region, identifying five key priority environmental subjects for which the sufficiency of national and regional laws can be measured. These five are illustrative of the challenges posed for regional cooperation through environmental law by all other environmental problems. They are:

(i) biodiversity conservation and natural and cultural heritage;
(ii) freshwater resources and forests;
(iii) marine and coastal resources;
(iv) human settlements; and
(v) the atmosphere.

The monograph's Chapter 4 examines the legal system of each state and evaluates its environmental laws and their efficacy. The constitution of each state is first examined for provisions on the environment. The chapter next ascertains the major multilateral environmental agreements (MEAs) that ASEAN member states have become a party to, and then examines the implementation of the obligations contained in these MEAs. The chapter finally assesses each state's own national laws, from the perspectives of the same five key areas mentioned above.

Chapter 5 traces the efforts at cooperation and collaboration within ASEAN, as well as with organizations outside ASEAN, while considering the gaps and obstacles along this path. It examines the approach of the ASEAN Way in the light of new and emerging challenges such as transnational environmental crimes, pandemic threats, transboundary pollution and climate change. It first considers the position pre-ASEAN Charter 2007 and then discusses the impact of the ASEAN Charter and beyond. The chapter discusses the implementation of the ASEAN Roadmap for an ASEAN Community 2009–2015 toward the attainment of the UN Millennium Development Goals. Case studies include the tackling of avian influenza, the Indonesian Haze, cyclone Nargis in Myanmar, the recent floods in Thailand and Typhoon Bopha in the Philippines, transnational environment crimes and the establishment of ASEAN-WEN as well as implementation of the ASEAN Strategic Plan of Action on Water Resources Management among the riparian states of the Mekong River.

Chapter 6 focuses on climate change and ASEAN's response. It is clear that climate change will have serious implications on biodiversity resources in the region, exacerbating poverty and accelerating biodiversity loss. ASEAN must foster greater collaboration among its member states to prepare for and adapt to the new environmental conditions. The impact of climate change is examined for each of the same five focus areas listed above in Chapter 4. It is likely that ASEAN's response to climate change, both at the regional and national levels and particularly in the context of adaptation to climate change ("think global, act local") will be crucial in determining whether ASEAN matures into a forceful regional authority for the coordination of mutual efforts to address common threats, or remains a useful but largely marginal force in regional collaborative action.

Chapter 7 concludes this monograph by reflecting on the challenges and highlighting several key areas for special focus. While concluding that integration through environmental law remains an ongoing "work in progress" in ASEAN, it is remarkable how considerable the progress has been since ASEAN's inception in 1967. The monograph ends on a positive note, because ASEAN cooperation for sustainability is clearly transcending ASEAN's early insistence on "non-interference" and is evolving. In doing so, ASEAN "builds foundations for peace and development."

Chapter 1

ASEAN and environmental sustainability

The Association of Southeast Asian Nations (ASEAN) aspires to be a neighborhood where richly diverse nations can attain common purposes by cooperating together in consensual and graduated steps. It proposes and posits "One Vision, One Identity, and One Caring and Sharing Community" as the uniting common ground.[1] Composed of ten sovereign states, ASEAN has at its core an international legal framework, through which it shapes its steps toward a shared vision. The goal of sustainable development, as articulated through the UN Conference on Environment and Development,[2] is a central vision shared by each ASEAN member state.

ASEAN cooperation on common policies and laws for the environment and development emerged through agreeing on topics of common concern, preparing draft

1 The ASEAN Charter, Jakarta, 2008, www.asean.org/archive/publications/ASEAN-Charter.pdf.

2 Agenda 21 is the product of the 1992 "Earth Summit," The UN Conference on Environment and Development (UNCED) held in Rio de Janeiro. UNCED also adopted the Declaration of Rio de Janeiro. Both these products of UNCED were thereafter endorsed by UN General Assembly resolutions. See www.un.org/esa/sustdev/documents/agenda21/index.htm. An annotated edition of Agenda 21 appears in the *traveaux préparatoires* for UNCED, N. A. Robinson et al., *Agenda 21 and the UNCED Proceedings*, 6 volumes (Oceana Publications, 1993).

programs that include capacity-building measures to ensure that each member state is ready to collaborate further, followed by the preparation of draft "soft law" policy declarations vetted through the appropriate governmental levels (civil service, ministers or heads of state). The soft law provides the basis for adopting congruent national laws and regulations to further a common ASEAN approach. In the environmental arena, this is well illustrated by the ASEAN biodiversity programs and the system of protected natural heritage areas.

The ASEAN Way builds confidence and avoids conflict among the member states. These goals are fundamental. War in Indochina raged through much of the twentieth century. As Principles 25 and 26 of the 1992 Rio Declaration on Environment and Development proclaim, "Warfare is inherently destructive of sustainable development. States shall therefore respect international law providing protection for the environment in times of armed conflict and cooperate in its further development, as necessary … Peace, development and environmental protection are interdependent and indivisible." ASEAN member states have identified cooperation in the field of environmental protection to be a common priority. Each has acknowledged the objective of sustainable development, as formulated by Agenda 21. Each is at a different point along the pathway to making development sustainable.

ASEAN perspectives on environmental sustainability cannot be separated from the history of each member state. Except for Thailand, each was colonized by states from outside the region. This left a legacy of civil law (with the Dutch, French or Spanish variants) and common law (with the British or American variants) and a legacy of Islamic legal principles and more recently socialist law principles, in the various states comprising ASEAN. Some concepts of nature conservation were indigenous to each nation, and these over-lays of foreign law in colonial times provided other conservation law models and natural resources development regimes.

Most conservation efforts were marginal to the dislocations and wars that marked the region and the time before the environment became an international priority, at the UN Conference on the Human Environment in Stockholm in 1972. It then took twenty years for the concept of sustainable development to take hold and for a fragile peace to emerge across the ASEAN region. By the time of the 1992 UN Conference on the Environment and Development (UNCED) in Rio de Janeiro, the definition of sustainable development as a goal took concrete form in Agenda 21, the consensus action plan. UNCED was chaired by Ambassador Professor Tommy Koh, of Singapore; he understood ASEAN well, and ASEAN provided distinguished leadership to the world through his role at UNCED and its preparatory committee.

Upon completion of UNCED, the ASEAN member states joined all other nations in approving Agenda 21 at the UN General Assembly, and then proceeded to fashion their own national Agenda 21 plans. Preparation of these national plans allowed policy-makers to study and come to apply

Agenda 21's diverse recommendations to their own national needs. Not all states had the immediate capacity to prepare a plan. For this reason Singapore assisted Myanmar in preparing its national plan. This process allowed ASEAN member states to develop a shared concept about what environmental sustainability might mean, and why it is important. From that common foundation, the states could then move to identify and develop the priorities for further analysis and action. In light of this timeline, it is fair to say that ASEAN member states have had less than two decades in which to integrate their legal systems toward the goals of environmental sustainability. This monograph describes a still youthful work in progress.

To coordinate their respective undertakings for building environmental sustainability, within each ASEAN member state the governments have enacted comparable environmental legislation, and established environmental ministries to advance the laws. Often the national laws are related to implementing a multilateral environmental agreement, such as the programs to reclaim and eliminate the chemicals that deplete the stratospheric ozone, under the 1985 Vienna Convention to Protect the Ozone Layer and the 1987 Montreal Protocol.[3] All ASEAN member states are parties to these treaties, and cooperate together. For example, Malaysia has won awards for its thorough implementation of the programs to eliminate ozone depleting substances,

[3] See http://ozone.unep.org/en/treaties-and-decisions for texts of agreements and ratifications, and implementing decisions of the conference and meetings of the state parties.

and worked to share its expertise with Indonesia and other nations.[4]

Once ASEAN member states agree on a theme for cooperation, they progressively define more specific measures and milestones in their agreed five-year plans of action, and adjust these as the participating authorities make progress and have reason to do so. The plans are pragmatic and flexible. Programs for sharing technical knowledge and building capacity are essential to reaching the point where environmental norms can be implemented. When ASEAN acts within this planning framework, it makes progress in using law as a tool for integration; laws can become measures for attaining measurable benchmarks of sustainability. This is environmental integration from within ASEAN. By contrast, when other institutions seek to marshal ASEAN member states from an external platform, such as the International Union for the Conservation of Nature and its 1985 ASEAN Agreement on the Conservation of Nature and Natural Resources,[5] or the UN Environment Programme (UNEP) and the ASEAN

[4] Paragraphs 40–7 in L. Kurukulasuriya and N. A. Robinson, *Training Manual on International Environmental Law* (UNEP, 2006) at pp. 106–7.

[5] IUCN's Environmental Law Programme sought to pattern the 1985 ASEAN Agreement on the successful African Convention on Conservation of Nature and Natural Resources, but the African Convention has a predecessor treaty for national parks and migration of wild animals among the colonial nations that governed Africa, and also the African states at independence had trained personnel accustomed to both national and transnational conservation practices. None of this existed in the ASEAN states. There was not yet a fertile substrata in which this agreement could become grounded and take

Agreement on Transboundary Haze Pollution (ATHP),[6] the lack of an ASEAN-wide process for building confidence and capacity has meant that it is more difficult for these regional agreements to enter into force. ASEAN member states do not wish to risk being in non-compliance with an agreement, since that might lead to disagreements and conflict; it is better to attain levels of compliance and then formalize these with acknowledgments and agreements *ex post facto*. However, considerable progress has been made as Indonesia finally ratified the ATHP Agreement in September 2014 – some twelve years after its signature, and was the last state to do so.[7]

root. Several states have ratified it, but others are needed before it can enter into force. Biodiversity management capacity across ASEAN has gained in capacity, and this may mean that the missing ratifications may be more realistic in the near future.

[6] The ATHP entered into force on November 25, 2003, after six ASEAN member states – Brunei Darussalam, Malaysia, Myanmar, Singapore, Thailand and Vietnam – ratified/acceded. Since then the Philippines and Cambodia have acceded to it. Indonesia finally ratified it in September 2014. UNEP's ASEAN Agreement on Transboundary Haze Pollution (2002) was meant to further a voluntary Regional Haze Action Plan of 1997, but it essentially involved the key states of Brunei, Indonesia, Malaysia and Singapore, and little effort was made to broaden its concerns to the other ASEAN member states. UNEP did not follow up the agreement with sustained capacity building, for example, in Indonesia. Had such capacity building been rooted in all ASEAN member states, incipient problems of the same sort among states such as Myanmar, Thailand, Vietnam, Lao PDR and Cambodia might have been addressed, and an ASEAN-wide consensus approach could have evolved and matured. This process remains to be cultivated.

[7] See www.straitstimes.com/news/asia/south-east-asia/story/indonesias-parliament-agrees-ratify-asean-haze-pact-20140916; and www.loc.gov/lawweb/servlet/lloc_news?disp3_l205404126_text.

Cooperation, consensus and capacity building characterize the methodology or approach of ASEAN integration through law as a means for building environmental protection and environmental sustainability. While the system works well, when it works, it must be acknowledged that as yet it is applied at a very modest scale compared to the burgeoning sustainability challenges in the region. For example, ASEAN does not yet address the deteriorating conditions of the extensive marine environment in the region, despite the acceptance by each ASEAN member state of the norm set out in Section 192 of the UN Convention on the Law of the Sea: "States have an obligation to protect and preserve the marine environment." The region still has vast areas where environmental marine degradation persists and even worsens. While ASEAN has established means by which to cooperate to remedy these problems, this work lies in the future.[8] One reason marine environmental protection is lacking may be because the UNEP took the lead in this area and has a broader reach than just the territorial waters and exclusive economic zones of the ASEAN member states,[9] and thus the scope for ASEAN internal marine cooperation has not been a prime focus of UNEP nor of

[8] See H. Kirkman, "The East Asian Seas UNEP Regional Seas Programme," (2006) 6 *International Agreements: Politics, Law and Economics* 3, pp. 305–16. See also the ASEAN Working Group on Coastal and Marine Environment (AWGCME) at http://environment.asean.org/46-2/.

[9] UNEP involves Australia, for example, and the cooperation is reviewed by the UNEP Governing Council and Global Environmental Facility (GEF) Council.

any regional seas programs.[10] Another reason may be that there are disputed territorial claims in the South China Sea that preclude negotiation of agreements on shared resource management.[11] Over-fishing in the archipelagos of Indonesia and the Philippines is depleting fish stocks relied upon for food. Despite the efforts of its Working Group on ASEAN Seas and Marine Environment, ASEAN's heads of state have not yet got to grips with safeguarding the region's seas.

As this monograph explains, building environmental policy and law has advanced integration among ASEAN member states toward shared concepts and practices for environmental sustainability. The region's challenge, however, is to meet the growing needs of people in each ASEAN nation in light of rapid population growth and the need to adapt to the physical impacts of climate disruption. As this monograph explains, at the current scale of its measures, ASEAN is not likely to meet its goals of attaining environmental sustainability. If it measurably scales up its efforts, then the ASEAN Way will have served to build a firm foundation for more extensive measures.

10 See the Report to the UNEP and GEF 2009, J. C. Pernetta, "Reversing Environmental Degradation Trends in the South China Sea and Gulf of Thailand" (Project No. GF/2730-02-4340, February 25, 2009).

11 China has overlapping territorial claims with four ASEAN states. See J.Tai, "Sino-US Rivalry Poses Challenges for ASEAN, Says Tommy Koh," *Straits Times*, December 19, 2012. See also "China's Maritime Disputes," www.cfr.org/asia-and-pacific/chinas-maritime-disputes/p31345#!/; and "Historical Fiction – China's South Sea Claims," May/June 2013, www.worldaffairsjournal.org/article/historical-fiction-china%E2%80%99s-south-china-sea-claims.

ASEAN has also sought to align its regional integration by cooperating with its "Dialogue Partners" and by entering into environmental agreements with Canada, India and the USA, among others. These provide ASEAN member states with confirmation that their environmental sustainability measures are in line with those of their major trading partners. These agreements facilitate the sharing of knowledge and best practices. ASEAN has been effective in collectively addressing transboundary and global environmental issues.[12] By aiming to apply comparable environmental policies and laws, ASEAN can level the playing field for trade within the region, and with other regions. Environmental externalities, which might produce economic advantages by allowing some parties to avoid the costs of combating pollution, can be curbed across all member states, providing benefits for both environment and trade. At the international level, ASEAN member states cooperate with the United Nations and with each other in disaster risk reduction, implementing the Hyogo Framework for Action (2005–2010), a voluntary system that builds capacity before it elaborates legal duties. The 5th Asian Ministerial Conference on Disaster Risk Reduction in Yogyakarta, Indonesia, in October 2012 spelled out a program for cooperation in building natural disaster preparedness.[13] ASEAN supports these international cooperation efforts because it already has confidence in its regional

[12] K.-L. Koh, "Transboundary and Global Environmental Issues: The Role of ASEAN," in *Transnational Environmental Law* (Cambridge University Press, 2012), doi:10.1017/S2047102511000082.

[13] See UN Office of Disaster Risk Reduction, www.unisdr.org.

disaster relief cooperation.[14] In a region prone to environmental and natural disasters, the need for states to cooperate and align their policies and laws is evident to most.

Environmental sustainability is also key to mutual security concerns. Sustainable development ensures that the new dimensions of "environmental security" can be met. Environmental security in the region varies from place to place, but invariably seeks to ensure that food is produced and available, that water is potable and available, that waste is not shipped across borders for illicit disposal and that forests or other flora and fauna are not exploited for commerce and depleted. Protecting the region against avian influenza, Severe Acute Respiratory Syndrome (SARS) or other diseases and phyto-sanitary threats, is a real concern across ASEAN. The military cannot provide collective security from the social and political problems that erupt from such threats; unsustainable practices exacerbate these dangers. In Indochina, these threats can spill over borders and produce refugees. With the rapid movement of people and goods, the archipelagic states are not immune from such problems either. ASEAN cooperation for environmental security is a new dimension of its work. The fact that ASEAN can plan for environmental security, a sensitive topic, is itself the result of successful cooperation on routine environmental issues, public health, education and trade.

ASEAN has grown from a skeletal secretariat with functional cooperation in six working groups led by different

[14] See ASEAN Agreement on Disaster Management and Emergency Response (AADMER), signed in Vientiane, 2005. See www.ahacentre.org/about-aadmer.

ministries from among ASEAN's member states, to a robust collaborative, network that is effectively integrating across the region, the services, programs, norms and legislation, and thus the law. The six working groups cover: (a) nature conservation, (b) ASEAN seas and the marine environment, (c) transboundary pollution, (d) environmental management, (e) environmental economics and (f) environmental information, public awareness and education. This collaborative approach ensures that expectations can be collectively arrived at, relied upon and agreed. These confidence-building systems enhance the rule of law.

ASEAN's success in deploying legal systems for building environmental sustainability is counter-intuitive to those who have a static concept of law-making, in which a treaty negotiation precedes national law implementation, or a legislative enactment precedes ministerial action to address an environmental issue. It must be acknowledged that the ASEAN Way described in this monograph is somewhat akin to a kind of *customary law*. The consensual practices and expected norms for behavior of the ASEAN Way are not embodied in an international agreement that is ratified and meets the characteristics of the Vienna Convention on the Law of Treaties. These norms are nonetheless known and observed and considered to be binding, although how they are to be observed varies from issue to issue. ASEAN is a regional undertaking, at once both intergovernmental and cultural or social. The ASEAN member states behave in the way they do because they have come to expect that this is required of a state in ASEAN, and if a state departs from the ASEAN Way, cooperation diminishes. This is not merely a question of weighing policy preferences, or a subject for behavioral studies by political or social scientists. The ASEAN Way itself has entered the realm of law. The modalities and mechanics of ASEAN cooperation should be recognized for what they have become: customary international law.[15]

The ASEAN Way involves decision by consensus, non-confrontational resolution of disputes and respect for the principles of sovereignty and non-intervention. On the whole, it makes for informality, quiet diplomacy, face-saving and an avoidance of legal instruments, that is, hard law. It is not unknown for there to have been departures from the ASEAN Way, particularly in the political context.[16] However, strict application of principles of sovereignty and non-intervention has been evident in the Indonesian Haze and in the aftermath of Cyclone Nargis – both discussed in Chapter 4.

[15] Paragraph 34 in L. Kurukulasuriya and N. A. Robinson, *Training Manual on International Environmental Law* (UNEP, 2006) at p. 7: "Once a rule of customary law is recognized, it is binding on all states. Because it is then assumed to be a binding rule of conduct. Initially, customary international law as we know it today developed in the context of the evolving interaction among European states. However, there is an increasingly prominent group of writers who suggest that other regions of the world also contributed to the evolution of customary international law." Within a defined transnational treaty system, such as that of ASEAN, there is scope for customary law to be recognized and applied, and deemed to be binding within those relationships. Such regional customary law is a body of law with a constant and uniform usage (*inveterate consuetudo*) and recognized that the behavior is required (*opinio juris*).

[16] L. Jones, *ASEAN, Sovereignty and Intervention in Southeast Asia* (Palgrave Macmillan, 2012).

In order to explore how ASEAN member states advance environmental sustainability through their "customary" law, informal "soft law" and more formal legal integration measures, the authors, in preparing this monograph, have consulted with environmental law experts in many of the ASEAN states. Their reports have augmented the authors' own research and helped to guide and inform this study. Law means different things in the various national cultures of the ASEAN states, and without comparative legal analysis one will fail to grasp what ASEAN legal integration entails. Those who would seek in this monograph purely formalistic analysis of legal institutions, statutes and treaties may be disappointed by our analysis. The positivists and legal realists may have difficulties in understanding "law" in this ASEAN context; those legal scholars who bring comparative law capacity, including a cultural and historical perspective, will be able to assess the nuanced roles that law plays in ASEAN environmental integration.

The authors of this monograph have each worked collaboratively across the ASEAN's dimensions in order to explore what they consider to be the fairly unique roles of customary and formal law-making in ASEAN, whether as hard or soft law. To access the realm of customary law, one needs to observe and partake of ASEAN decision-making, and be involved in it, in order to understand and assess it.[17]

[17] See K.-L. Koh, compiler and editor, *ASEAN Environmental Law, Policy and Governance, Selected Documents*, vol. I (World Scientific, 2009) at p. 713; ibid., vol. II (World Scientific, 2012) at p. 1371. Each of the authors has been privileged to have participated at workshops and conferences where ASEAN environmental law has been discussed,

This monograph offers a suggestive methodology for other scholars who may also wish to enter into the exploration of ASEAN and law, or for the study of ITL in other regional settings.

Professors Koh and Lye being citizens of an ASEAN member state, Singapore, and Professor Robinson as an environmental law specialist by invitation. Koh has presented papers on ASEAN in numerous international conferences, seminars and workshops. She was invited to conduct a series of lectures on ASEAN environmental law at the Law Faculty of Universidad Metropolitana de Mexico; the Richardson School of Law, Hawaii; and the Syriah Kula University, Aceh, Indonesia. Koh and Lye have jointly taught courses on ASEAN environmental law and the environmental law of Southeast Asia for many years at NUS. Robinson and Koh have co-authored papers on ASEAN's environmental law.

Chapter 2

Integrating sustainability into ASEAN state practice

> ASEAN is not only a well-functioning indispensable reality in the region. It is a real force to be reckoned with far beyond the region. It is also a trusted partner of the United Nations in the field of development.
>
> Kofi Annan, former Secretary-General of the United Nations (February 16, 2000)

Since the United Nations General Assembly accepted the Report from the World Commission on Environment and Development, entitled *Our Common Future* (1987),[1] environmentally sustainable development has evolved to become a central theme for ASEAN.[2] The documentation of this evolutionary progress appears in *ASEAN Environmental Law, Policy and Governance: Selected Documents* compiled by Koh

[1] Known also as the "Brundtland Report," www.un-documents.net/wced-ocf.htm.

[2] These developments have been noted. See also N. A. Robinson and K.-L. Koh, "Regional Environmental Governance: Examining the Association of Southeast Asian Nations (ASEAN) Model," in D. C. Esty and M. H. Ivanova (eds.), *Global Environmental Governance: Options & Opportunities* (Yale University Press, 2002); K.-L. Koh and Md. S. Karim, "South East Asian Environmental Legal Governance," in S. Alam, J. Hossain Bhuiyan, T. Chowdhury and E. Techera (eds.), *Routledge Handbook of International Environmental Law* (Routledge Taylor & Francis Group, 2012), pp. 461–77.

Kheng-Lian. This body of state practice is substantial. The key measures that illustrate patterns of integration through law (ITL) have been usefully analyzed and collected into two readily available compendia – the first volume,[3] Part I, "Setting the Stage for ASEAN Environmental Cooperation, Harmonization, and Integration" and Part II, "General Legal Frameworks on the Environment," which contains ASEAN documents on environmental law. These environmental legal instruments appear not only in the ASEAN Socio-Cultural Community Blueprint (also known as the Third Pillar) but across the ASEAN Political Security Community Blueprint (also known as the First Pillar). Volume I also includes documents setting forth ASEAN's environmental Programmes, Strategies, Plans of Action and Blueprints, as well as Declarations, Resolutions and Accords. The second volume[4] focuses on specific sectors such as terrestrial ecosystems – natural resources and biodiversity; coastal and marine environment; water resources management; health and environment; energy and climate change; disaster management; environmental education; and ASEAN environmental governance. Both volumes should be considered companions to the commentaries in this monograph.

It is beyond the scope of this study to address each of the many ASEAN environmental decision-making processes

[3] K.-L. Koh, compiler and editor, *ASEAN Environmental Law, Policy and Governance, Selected Documents*, vol. I (World Scientific, 2009), also available in an electronic edition 978-981-4261-19-7.

[4] K.-L. Koh, compiler and editor, *ASEAN Environmental Law, Policy and Governance, Selected Documents*, vol. II (World Scientific, 2012), also available in an electronic edition, 978-981-4329-59-0.

that constitute environmental law, policy and governance in ASEAN. This monograph will selectively reference ASEAN decision-making documents where relevant to an analysis of the rule of law in ASEAN integration, from an environmental law perspective. It should be noted that not all areas that need environmental integration are as yet amenable to integration for reasons of politics, sensitivity of issues, lack of knowledge and capacity, or other reasons.

Evaluating how environmental law functions in the context of ASEAN "integration" can be challenging because the realm of the environment is all encompassing. The environment is not a single sector, but its elements are embedded in all of the ASEAN pillars and engagements. The vast scope of environmental decision-making within so many sectors presents exceptionally difficult challenges for those studying ASEAN. It is essential to examine traditional areas of governance such as public health, trade, education, power generation and distribution, ports, marine resources, nature conservation and biodiversity, farming, industrial pollution, hazardous waste and military security. In addition, the gathering menace of climate change requires analysis of disaster preparedness, flood control and water resource management, and adaptation to sea-level rises and storm surge.

Mature environmental law systems establish and employ "Environmental Management Systems" (EMS) to provide an overview of how these sectors interrelate and to integrate management responses. Efficient allocation of scarce budgetary and human resources across the regimes of environmental legislation requires EMS. This can be done within a nation through a cabinet-level committee or an office directly under the prime minister or president in a government, or chief executive officer in a company. As a step leading up to this most efficient governance model, most states establish an environment ministry (often combining several related functions) or have an environmental compliance or sustainable development department in a company. In ASEAN, it is these governmental focal points that meet together to study, design and recommend new ASEAN-wide policies, programs or strategies for adoption by ministers and ultimately heads of state.

In this monograph, the concept of "integration" is not used in a narrow or legally technical sense.[5] ITL is a complex area of legal scholarship. ASEAN integration through environmental law requires that each nation has a stable national and local rule of law system. It must have systems to expose and root out corruption, and a functioning legislative process to enact environmental laws. It requires a stable environmental regulatory regime, usually administered through an executive ministry or offices mandated with the responsibility to implement specified environmental laws. Chief among the national legal systems for building sustainable development is the "Environmental Impact Assessment" (EIA), mandated by Principle 17 of the

[5] The *Oxford Dictionary* defines integration as "the action or process of integrating i.e. the intermixing of people or groups previously segregated." *Black's Law Dictionary* (9th edn, 2009) defines integration as "1. The process of making whole or combining into one. 2. Contracts. The full expression of the parties' agreement, so that all earlier agreements are superseded, the effect being that neither party may later contradict or add to the contractual terms."

Rio Declaration on Environment and Development[6] and contained in Article 14 of the ASEAN Agreement on the Conservation of Nature and Natural Resources (1985)[7] and Article 14 of the UN Convention on Biological Diversity (CBD). To ensure EIAs and other environmental legislation function as intended, states need to have in place governance systems to implement Principle 10 of the Rio Declaration:

> Environmental issues are best handled with the participation of all concerned citizens, at the relevant level. At the national level, each individual shall have appropriate access to information concerning the environment that is held by public authorities, including information on hazardous materials and activities in their communities, and the opportunity to participate in decision-making processes. States shall facilitate and encourage public awareness and participation by making information widely available. Effective access to judicial

[6] Principle 17 states: "Environmental impact assessment, as a national instrument, shall be undertaken for proposed activities that are likely to have a significant adverse impact on the environment and are subject to a decision of a competent national authority."

[7] Article 14 states: "(1) The Contracting Parties undertake that proposals for any activity which may significantly affect the natural environment shall as far as possible be subjected to an assessment of their consequences before they are adopted, and they shall take into consideration the results of this assessment in their decision-making process.(2) In those cases where any such activities are undertaken, the Contracting Parties shall plan and carry them out so as to overcome or minimize any assessed adverse effects and shall monitor such effects with a view to taking remedial action as appropriate." However, this Agreement is still not in force, pending ratification by three signatories.

> and administrative proceedings, including redress and remedy, shall be provided.[8]

The implementation of international environmental agreements and the multilateral environmental agreements (MEAs) in turn also depends on having an effective national environmental law regime. The MEAs have the effect of harmonizing norms and standards across all nations, including those of the ASEAN region, but the realization of the MEAs depends on effective national regimes as the building blocks of the international systems. ASEAN has played a significant role in the facilitation of the implementation of MEAs, both within Southeast Asia and as a contribution by that region to patterns of international cooperation.

Analysis of the national environmental law regimes in each of the ASEAN nations is essential to understanding how integration through law has progressed with respect to environmental protection.[9] In addition to consulting with scholars in many ASEAN states, the authors have compared the national laws in ASEAN with those in other regions; these comparisons are evaluated in Chapter 4. Comparative analysis reveals an uneven pattern of environmental law in each country. Key elements for the rule of law and for the legal foundations for sustainable development are missing in many nations of the ASEAN community. The EIA, even

[8] Rio Principle 10, The Rio Declaration on Environment and Development, UNGA Res. 47/190 (1992).

[9] See, for example, the collections of national laws available through ECOLEX, a database of UNEP, IUCN and the UN Food and Agriculture Organization.

where in use, is often weakly applied. Systems for ensuring access to environmental information, public participation and justice remain at rudimentary levels in some member states, and at very advanced levels in others. Accordingly, capacity building is needed to bring each nation to a level where they can implement ASEAN environmental policies evenly across all member states. It is because of this reality that ASEAN programs and five-year plans stress capacity building as a priority. Both sustainable development and the rule of law depend on capacity building.

When analyzing ASEAN ITL it is necessary to examine two distinct but interrelated aspects of integration: (a) institutional integration and (b) integration of laws and policies. Both aspects are elements of a systems approach to evaluating environmental governance. Chapter 5 of this study evaluates the gaps in these integration aspects of ASEAN's regional and national environmental governance systems to measure the progress and prospects for ITL in ASEAN.

Whatever the current or future capacity of ASEAN and its member states to advance sustainable development through environmental law, the region is not yet ready to handle the impacts of climate change. Chapter 6 examines these challenges. All national and regional environmental stewardship, and the rule of law itself, will be tested enormously as the regions respond to storm frequency and severity and other climatic impacts, such as sustained droughts and sea-level rise. ASEAN, like all regional integration organizations, will need to strengthen legal and governance systems for interstate cooperation and collaboration. ASEAN has already begun to do this in response to zoonotic diseases, such as avian influenza or SARS, for which societies become more vulnerable through the effects of climate change.

ASEAN has established an enviable record of region-wide collaboration in the stewardship of the region's biological diversity, particularly its terrestrial biodiversity. Because the region's systems for protecting nature and parks, and for sustaining biodiversity, are at a relatively advanced stage, ASEAN policies for nature conservation are given specific attention. It should be noted that in protecting nature, the benefits of natural area conservation have enhanced the capacity of human communities to cope with the effects of climate change. Conserving water catchment areas and forests prevents floods, while ensuring fresh water supplies. Establishing marine protected areas conserves the food chain for fish while providing a basis for coping with a sea-level rise. Saving or re-establishing mangroves and wetlands safeguards upland areas from flood surges. Even where ASEAN has not established biodiversity programs to immediately address these ecosystem services and benefits, member states do derive benefits. Cooperative measures to protect the peat bogs and wetlands for biodiversity purposes, and to contain their methane deposits in order to mitigate the release of methane and climate change, can bring collateral benefits as they end the burning of such areas and help resolve the regional "haze" problems that affect Indonesia, Malaysia and Singapore. Biodiversity stewardship in ASEAN furthers sustainable development and cooperation among its member states.

Perhaps more importantly from an ITL perspective the member states have learned how to cooperate and learn from one another, how to build and implement programs for biodiversity and enhance the legal frameworks for doing so. This is a major, if little-acknowledged contribution of ASEAN and its environmental endeavors. ASEAN is succeeding in showing its member states how to build resilience in each nation, both for immediate needs of sustainable development and biodiversity conservation, and for future needs associated with the impacts of climate change. Above all, there is evidence that ITL is happening, which bodes well for mutual aid in coping with environmental disasters or unexpected challenges to sustainable development programs.

How ASEAN may enhance its ITL, meet its challenges and fulfill its prospects is the subject of Chapter 7 of this study. One cannot divorce ASEAN from its member states, and vice versa. They share a common interdependence on the region's natural resources. Building a culture of shared expectations and goals, through a kind of proto-law or "soft law" and policy, is absolutely essential to consensus decision-making. Building an "ASEAN identity" – a theme addressed in Chapter 1 – returns in Chapter 4 as an important prerequisite to ASEAN community, regional cooperation and mutual aid. A shared valuing of cultural and natural heritage – resources that are unique to the history and geography of each nation – is a unifying force in ASEAN.[10] Their conservation brings pride and

[10] Some controversies surrounding cultural heritage sites are: Angkor Wat in Cambodia (a claim by a Thai actress that the site belonged to Thailand led to a series of riots) and the Preah Vihear temple (Cambodia and Thailand each lay claims to the site). See *Case Concerning the Temple of Preah Vihear (Cambodia* v. *Thailand)* at www.icj-cij.org/docket/files/45/4871.pdf.

tourism and a sense of an ASEAN-wide community. Even a nation behind in sustainable development, such as Myanmar, is rich in culture, and ASEAN can embrace and magnify this heritage regionally and globally.

Since ASEAN is a dynamic and evolving association of rapidly developing nations, and environmental law-making is an urgent and ongoing process, it is likely that the descriptions provided in this monograph of the environmental laws of each ASEAN member state will become out of date, rapidly. On the other hand, the ASEAN Way is to build cooperation across the member states incrementally, and by consensus, so this body of state practice grows incrementally and the legal analysis may be useful over a longer period of time. The ASEAN patterns of environmental cooperation are exceedingly robust and growing in support in each ASEAN member state.

This study, then, offers an assessment of where the national implementation of ASEAN environmental goals stands as of April 1, 2015, two decades after the Rio Earth Summit encouraged ASEAN to make sustainable development a foundation of its work. It is likely that in another two decades, environmental law across ASEAN nations will have evolved to reflect a distinctive ASEAN character. Given the challenges of a growing population and increasing climate change impacts throughout the ASEAN region, the promise of environmental law to sustain the resilience of human and natural systems is intertwined into each of ASEAN's three pillars. ITL will help sustain those pillars.

Chapter 3

The environment in the ASEAN region

> Evergreen tropical forests, mountain forests, monsoon forests, limestone and karst formations, wetlands, marine and coastal waters – these are among the major habitats or ecosystems found in Southeast Asia that store the world's largest collection of plant and animal life. These are life-giving resources for over half a billion people of the region and millions more around the world.[1]
>
> Dr. Surin Pitsuwan, ASEAN Secretary-General

3.1 Evaluating bio-geographic trends in the ASEAN region

Members of ASEAN share a common appreciation of nature in their customs, religious beliefs and social values. They also share the experiences of rapid urbanization and growing national populations. From 450 million in 1990, more than 622 million people live in ASEAN's ten countries in 2012, soon to be an estimated 650 million by 2020. Human population growth is most rapid in Indonesia (40 percent), the Philippines (17 percent) and Vietnam (16 percent), and

[1] S. Pitsuwan, "Message from the ASEAN Director-General," in ASEAN Centre for Biodiversity, *The ASEAN Heritage Parks: A Journey to the Natural Wonders of Southeast Asia* (Dolmar Press, 2010), p. iii.

the demands on environmental resources grow commensurately. All people among member states rely on the environment for their livelihoods, whether directly or indirectly. Despite disparities in levels of socio-economic development, with gross domestic product per person ranging from US$59,937 to US$1,327,[2] member states collaborate to identify what is needed for environmental protection and the attainment of sustainable development.[3] They cooperate through five-year planning cycles to build their capacity to provide environmental protection as a pillar for socio-economic development.[4] Member states have made significant gains in building their capacity to be stewards of nature and natural resources, and to implement regionally their national obligations under multilateral environmental agreements

[2] K. Brown, "A Fragmented Forum," *Financial Times*, November 25, 2011, p. 9: The GDP per head of ASEAN members at 2011 purchasing parity is: Singapore, US$59,937; Brunei, US$49,518; Malaysia, US$15,579; Thailand, US$9,693; Indonesia, US$4,668; Philippines, US$4,111; Vietnam, US$3,355; Lao PDR, US$2,659; Cambodia, US$2,286 and Myanmar, US$1,327. See also Kishore Mahbubani and Rhoda Severino "ASEAN: The Way Forward," May 2014, www.mckinsey.com/insights/public_sector/asean_the_way_forward.

[3] This intergovernmental environmental legal and policy integration has been noted for some time. See, for example, N. A. Robinson and K.-L. Koh, "Regional Environmental Governance: Examining the Association of Southeast Asian Nations (ASEAN) Model," in D. C. Esty and M. H. Ivanova (eds.), *Global Environmental Governance: Options & Opportunities* (Yale University Press, 2002).

[4] ASEAN member states support the Declaration of Johannesburg of 2002, confirming that environmental protection is an equal pillar of sustainable development, along with the economic and social (cultural) pillars. Johannesburg Declaration on Sustainable Development, UN Doc. A/CONF. 1999/L.6/Rev.3, 4 September 2002.

and other environmental treaties.[5] Nonetheless, as ASEAN's Secretary-General acknowledges:

> The environmental performance of most ASEAN Member States, as assessed by reputable studies, is above the world average, and the ecological footprint is much lower than that of many nations. However, ASEAN will continue to face growing environmental challenges given the need to lift a third of its population earning less than $2 a day out of poverty, and the many other pressures exerted on the environment such as population growth, urbanization and industrialization.[6]

Law provides both a significant foundation and an effective procedure for ASEAN member states as they pursue intergovernmental environmental cooperation. The ASEAN Way encourages the sharing of goals and agreement by consensus on a phased pacing of capacity building for environmental stewardship, as discussed in Chapter 5 of this study. This approach builds goodwill, is based on actual, objectively verified assessments of needs in ways that avert embarrassment and saves face. This approach is aimed ultimately at implementing the ASEAN Charter's goals: "ASEAN shall be united by a common desire and collective will to live in a

[5] The multilateral environmental agreements and other international agreements are collected in L. Kurukulasuriya and N. A. Robinson, *Training Manual on International Environmental Law* (UNEP, 2006). Most ASEAN members have ratified or acceded to most of the environmental agreements that harmonize state obligations under international law. See NUS Centre for International Law at http://cil.nus.edu.sg/2009/cil-documents-database/.

[6] S. Pitsuwan, 'Foreword' in Fourth ASEAN State of the Environment Report, 2009, p. iii.

region of lasting peace, security and stability, sustained economic growth, shared prosperity and social progress."[7] The ASEAN concept of sustainable development is expressed in ASEAN Vision 2020: "A clean and green ASEAN with fully established mechanisms for sustainable development to ensure the protection of the region's environment, the sustainability of natural resources and a high quality of life of its peoples."[8] In 2009, ASEAN adopted a "Roadmap for an ASEAN Community 2009–2015" to promote sustainable development, including the greening of the ASEAN economy.[9]

While member states have agreed to a common environmental agenda in five-year plans since 1978, the establishment of national legal frameworks necessary to realize the agenda reveals shortcomings. Most states have agreed to adopt the same multilateral and international treaty obligations to protect the environment, and thus have enacted comparable national legislation needed to implement their respective duties under international law. The administration of these laws, however, is uneven at best. As Chapter 4 of this study illustrates, the state of national environmental legal systems to implement agreements and legislation varies from nation to nation. This is not merely a differentiation based

[7] ASEAN Charter (November 20, 2007), which entered into force on December 15, 2008.

[8] ASEAN Vision 2020, Kuala Lumpur, December 15, 1997. The agreement can be found at www.aseansec.org/1814.htm.

[9] Association of Southeast Asian Nations, Roadmap for an ASEAN Community 2009–2015, 2009, www.meti.go.jp/policy/trade_policy/east_asia/dl/ASEANblueprint.pdf.

on levels of socio-economic development. All the ASEAN member states have some problems in common. Within each nation, large cities command priorities for environmental services, and in regions distant from cities and capitals, the supply of environmental services or the regulation of natural resources is often lacking. Most nations have extensive parks and protected areas, important resources for ecotourism and biodiversity, but at the same time most lack the capacity to manage air and water pollution, and to prevent transboundary pollution.

ASEAN's gradually consensual and deliberate form of cooperation seems to preclude rapid response to environmental problems across the states. Moreover, when a member state would prefer not to give priority to solving an environmental problem, for whatever reason, it simply avoids ratifying or adhering to regional agreements that other member states have ratified. This is the case with the Agreement on Conservation of Nature and Natural Resources[10] and the ASEAN Agreement on Transboundary Haze Pollution.[11] Other than cooperating to build overall capacity in the field of environmental protection, there is no ASEAN central

[10] ASEAN Agreement on the Conservation of Nature and Natural Resources, Kuala Lumpur, July 9, 1985. The Agreement can be found at www.aseansec.org/1490.htm. It was signed by the first six state parties, ratified by only three and thus is still not in force many years later.

[11] This was signed by all ten states in June 2002, and was ratified by all states except Indonesia, which finally ratified in late 2014. See www.asean.org/news/asean-secretariat-news/item/indonesia-deposits-instrument-of-ratification-of-the-asean-agreement-on-transboundary-haze-pollution.

bureaucracy to mandate or encourage all member states to implement such agreements. The political process at the level of heads of state may need to address this aspect of future ASEAN decision-making for strengthening sustainable development.

Like many other aspects of ASEAN efforts at regional integration, ASEAN's environmental component is a work in progress. Much has been done, but as an assessment of the region's environmental challenges makes evident, much more remains to be done. The new threats associated with climate change, outlined in Chapter 6 of this study, compound the difficulties that ASEAN will have across all of its environmental and economic integration. The environment of Southeast Asia is complex, with problems associated with different sectors. Externalities from the region's "tiger economies" and sprawling cities, expanding commercial agriculture and growing industrial capabilities combine to necessitate better laws and administrative regimes to abate air and water pollution, and to contain and control hazardous wastes. The growing exploitation of fish, forests and all renewable natural resources requires management systems for ensuring that yields can be sustained; too often exploitation proceeds at unsustainable levels and these resources face depletion. Deforestation not only depletes forests, but erodes soils, unleashes flood waters and reduces biodiversity. Agricultural sectors are often left to their own devices, with insufficient exchange of best management practices and loss of important agricultural areas through conversion to other developmental uses. The rapid loss of peat wetlands in Indonesia through conversion to palm oil plantations is one example of this problem. Urban water supplies are lacking and potable water supplies are impaired in many urban and even rural areas. Extinction of species, including the loss of rare corals, is a phenomenon across the region. Scientists in the region have assessed these trends and identified the need for more concerted action by ASEAN and others.[12]

The environmental challenges throughout ASEAN's region can be surveyed to set the scene for examining how law is integrating (or failing to integrate) ASEAN member states into a region-wide legal system for environmental protection and sustainable development. Since 1997, ASEAN itself has assessed the "State of the Environment" in periodic reports, every three years.[13] It is an indicator of the maturity of ASEAN's environmental systems that they benchmark and assess their environmental problems. Based on these ASEAN

[12] L. Lebel, A. Snidvongs, C. T. A. Chen and R. Daniel (eds.), *Critical States: Environmental Challenges to Development in Monsoon Southeast Asia* (Strategic Information and Research Development Centres, 2009). See also the South Asia Regional Committee (SARCS) for the Global System for Analysis Research and Training (START) at www.sarcs.org.

[13] See, for example, the Fourth ASEAN State of the Environment Report, 2009, available in CD ROM, in 3 volumes: 1. Environment – ASEAN; 2. Natural Resources – Economics; 3. Natural Development – Consumption. Jakarta, ASEAN Secretariat, 2009. The first report includes the seven nation members of ASEAN in 1997; three years later the report included the then ten nations in ASEAN, In 2002, the ASEAN submitted a report to the 2002 UN Summit on Sustainable Development in South Africa, which served as a comparable assessment, and the Third ASEAN State of the Environment Report was delayed until 2006. The fourth report appeared in 2009. A fifth report is expected.

reports, and the reports that member states contribute to other intergovernmental organizations such as the Conferences of the Parties for the UN Framework Convention on Climate Change (UNFCCC)[14] and the UN Convention on Biological Diversity (CBD),[15] or the United Nations' Commission on Sustainable Development (CSD),[16] it is possible to identify several priority areas of environmental concern across the entire ASEAN region. The empirical and acknowledged accounts of the region's environmental problems, in turn, provide a basis for assessing how environmental law and the rule of law are essential to ecological and socio-economic development throughout ASEAN. Despite the availability of information about the environmental trends in ASEAN, and the well-documented knowledge of specific problems, such as the "haze" that affects Malaysia and Singapore as a result of burning biomass in Indonesia, the ASEAN State of the Environment Reports tend not to report on critical problems. The ASEAN Way guides what is reported and how, apparently because of the political sensitivities among ASEAN member states and the lack of agreement on how to prioritize and resolve the problems.

Analysis of scientific and policy literature about the environment in Southeast Asia permits selection of several

[14] See National Reports to UNFCCC at http://unfccc.int/national_reports/items/1408.

[15] See National Reports to the CBD Secretariat at www.cbd.int/reports/.

[16] See submission by Singapore and submission by Thailand for the UN Conference on Sustainable Development at www.uncsd2012.org/comp_memberstates.html.

important environmental challenges. Five broad environmental themes may be featured here to illustrate how ASEAN treats law and environmental sustainability. Each theme affords insights into an objective, factual context against which the sufficiency of national and regional environmental law may be measured, assessed and benchmarked. After broadly sketching an introduction to the unique and richly diverse Southeast Asian environment, the following issues can be described in summary fashion: (a) biodiversity, natural heritage and cultural heritage;[17] (b) freshwater resources and forests;[18] (c) marine and coastal resources;[19] (d) human

17 The UNESCO World Heritage Convention and the International Union for Conservation of Nature (IUCN) World Commission on Protected Areas (WCPA) provide an international framework for ASEAN regional cooperation, as does the multilateral environmental agreements (MEAs) UN Convention on Biological Diversity. ASEAN member states have signed and ratified these agreements, and the EU has provided a capacity-building ASEAN Biodiversity Centre located in the Philippines. The IUCN's ASEAN Agreement on the Conservation of Nature and Natural Resources is not yet in force.

18 Mostly national law governs this area. The International Tropical Timber Organization deals with commerce in timber; UN Forest Principles are voluntary; there is little on freshwater, other than the Mekong River Agreement. See Agreement on the Cooperation for the Sustainable Development of the Mekong River Basin, April 5, 1995. The Agreement can be found at www.mrcmekong.org/assets/Publications/policies/agreement-Apr95.pdf. Lacking international law, ASEAN decision-making is important in this sphere.

19 United Nations Convention on the Law of the Sea (UNCLOS) applies in the region as a background law; see Article XII on the environment. See also the UN Environmental Programme Action Plan for the Protection and Development of the Marine and Coastal Areas of the East Asian Region, April 1981, at www.cobsea.org/; and UN Agreement

settlements[20] and (e) the atmosphere.[21] With respect to each theme, the major governing environmental law is at the national level. Therefore, evidence of regional integration through national legislation and with ASEAN decision-making can be identified and contrasted. For example, the prevention and response to zoonotic diseases implicate human settlements, where humans contract the diseases and need medical care, with biological diversity management, where the disease vectors need to be contained. Human commerce and trade are also disease vectors. Comparable intersectoral aspects appear when environmental disaster management and responses are studied, as noted above. Food and fuel for human settlements entails setting sustainability norms for fishing, agriculture and waste management, as pollution is invariably a transboundary as well as a local phenomenon.

for the Implementation of the Provisions of UNCLOS Relating to the Conservation and Management of Straddling Fish Stocks and Highly Migratory Fish Stocks, A/CONF.164/27, September 8, 1995. These laws set the framework within which ASEAN decision-making advances.

20 Most national laws deal with cities and countryside settlements. The UN HABITAT Programme is mandated by the United Nations General Assembly to promote socially and environmentally sustainable towns and cities with the goal of providing adequate shelter for all. This is an important area for ASEAN decision-making with little international law relevant.

21 The UNFCCC Climate Treaty is in force, but not much has been implemented other than a few clean development mechanism (CDM) projects under Kyoto. The Geneva Convention on Long Range Transboundary Air Pollution does not apply to acid rain in the region; the UNEP ASEAN Haze Treaty is now in force. National air pollution laws are the main legal focus, and ASEAN decision-making can address this sphere with little international law applicable.

It must be acknowledged that much more attention could be devoted to degradation of the marine environment. The mass of ocean exceeds the mass of land in ASEAN's region. The marine environment is at significant risk, particularly coral reefs.[22] Mangroves, seagrass, salt water or tidal wetlands and fisheries are similarly of great concern. Currently, it must be admitted that most ASEAN member states do not have effective controls for land-based sources of marine pollution. Tremendous volumes of liquid waste enter the oceans from discharges into rivers and bays. As fisheries decline across the ASEAN region, it is likely that priorities will emerge favoring cooperation on the marine environment. The protection of the marine environment is not considered unimportant, but ASEAN's record of coping with marine resources largely remains to be developed. It should

[22] See, for example, L.-M. Chou, "Challenges to Southeast Asia's Status as the Global Coral Reef Hotspot," in V. R. Savage and L.-H. Lye, *Environment and Climate Change in Asia: Ecological Footprints and Green Prospects* (Pearson, 2011). See the work of the ASEAN Working Group on Coastal and Marine Environment. It adopted the ASEAN Marine Water Quality Criteria in 2002, based on seventeen parameters, and also completed a publication on Marine Protected Areas in Southeast Asia, developed by the ASEAN Centre for Biodiversity – to provide a reference for policy-makers, planners, academia and park managers on the management of marine protected areas in order to save, rehabilitate and safeguard the coastal and marine resources in the region. With support from the ASEAN Centre for Biodiversity, the working group has also undertaken the development of both offline and online interfaces for encoding (i) species and (ii) protected areas. The offline and online database is expected to facilitate information sharing among ASEAN member states. See http://environment.asean.org/46-2/.

be acknowledged that ASEAN's record is roughly the same as most other coastal marine regions. The obligation in the Convention on the Law of the Sea to "protect" the oceans remains aspirational worldwide.

3.2 The state of the environment in the ASEAN region and five key issues

Before examining how each of the ASEAN member states addresses the five themes identified in Section 3.1 on a national and ASEAN level, it is instructive to describe selected issues characterizing the state of the environment in the ASEAN region.[23]

The ASEAN region is a vast region, 3,300 km from north to south and 5,600 km from west to east, and home to 20 percent of all the world's species in ecosystems found in lakes, rivers, seas, forests and mountains.[24] Three mega-diverse states – Indonesia, Malaysia and the Philippines – share ASEAN's region with the five mainland riverine systems of the Mekong River and Delta, Chao Phraya, Irrawaddy, Red

[23] See the Fourth ASEAN State of the Environment Report, 2009, Jakarta (2009). The report can be found at www.aseansec.org/publications/SoER4-Report.pdf. Additional statistics can be found in The World Factbook (2014) at www.cia.gov/library/publications.the-world-factbook/.

[24] The region includes bio-geographical features that cross national borders, such as the Malaysian, Wallacea, Indo-Burma and Central Indo-Pacific. There is a large body of scientific literature about these regions. For purposes of this study, the environmental reports compiled to address more focused intergovernmental topics are relied upon.

and Salween rivers within the states of Cambodia, Lao PDR, Myanmar, Thailand and Vietnam (comprising 1,940,100 km^2). The Mekong River alone drains a watershed of 795,000 km^2, and rises in China. Within its marine waters, ASEAN holds the world's most diverse marine species and comprises one-third of the world's coral reefs – all within 284,000 km^2.[25] The region has 173,000 km of coastline, and the ASEAN region extends into the South China Sea, the Andaman Sea, the Philippine Sea, the Gulf of Thailand and the Gulf of Tonkin. Maritime Southeast Asia, or the Malay Archipelago, is composed of Brunei Darussalam, Indonesia, Sabah and Sarawak (East Malaysia), the Philippines and Singapore.

The extraordinary natural and ancient cultural monuments of the ASEAN region make it an important destination for ecotourism. Except during the periods of health concerns due to the SARS and the avian influenza, and episodes of transboundary air pollution from forest fires in Indonesia, tourism has been increasing in the region. Malaysia, Singapore and Thailand provide tourism infrastructure for the mainland area of ASEAN, where tourism volumes are a growing and important part of the service economy.

Situated in a monsoon region, the tropical climate nations experience rainfall between 1,000 to 4,000 mm each

[25] The ASEAN Centre for Biodiversity, supported also by the European Union, and located in the Philippines, facilitates cooperation among ASEAN members in collecting and sharing data on biodiversity and building capacity to avert the decline or extinction of species and their habitats. See www.aseanbiodiversity.org/.

year. The Northeast Monsoon (November to March) brings abundant rains; the Southwest Monsoon in the months of May to September brings stronger, dry winds and extends the range of air pollutants. The monsoons supply the needs of the region's people, farming and natural areas. The El Niño climate fluctuations build some uncertainty into seasonal rainfalls and, in cities, the urban growth has outpaced the capacity to handle floodwaters. The ASEAN region has 8.7 percent of the world's human population, and the region's population will grow from 580 to 650 million by 2020, with an average density of 132 people per km^2 (as opposed to a world average of 50.6 people).[26] Megacities such as Jakarta and Metro-Manila have 10,000 people per km^2. As of 2005, 44 percent of the people in ASEAN lived in cities. The region became important as a trading corridor between 500 and 1500 CE,[27] and continues to be an important trading region today.

Farming and fishing employ large numbers and supply food to local populations. Agriculture is more important than macro-economic trade indicators may suggest, for local farming and fishing supply the essential food needs of local populations and employ large numbers of people. Crops across ASEAN include the following: rice, maize, soy bean, and cassava (Indonesia), rice (Myanmar), maize and sugar cane (the Philippines), rice, sugar and cassava (Thailand) and rice and sugar cane (Vietnam). Agriculture specialization

[26] World Population Prospects, the 2012 Revision (last updated June 13 2013): http://esa.un.org/wpp/documentation/publications.htm.

[27] S. Gordon, *When Asia Was the World* (De Capo Press, 2009).

has recognized values for trade, with exports of palm oil ($10 billion in 2006) and crude rubber ($12 billion) being significant. According to the UN Food and Agricultural Organization, forest cover decreased from 53.4 percent to 41.9 percent between 1993 and 1994, the result of deforestation for lumber and to clear land for agriculture. This trend continues. Agricultural lands increased from 17.4 percent to 24.7 percent in the same period.[28]

The ASEAN region is dependent on imports of oil and gas for much of the region's energy supplies. Brunei, Indonesia and Malaysia produce oil and refine it, and Singapore imports oil and refines it. ASEAN policy promotes establishing green energy systems, but rather little has been installed as yet. The region's legal and development administrative systems continue to favor large dams or large fossil fuel electrical generating installations. Energy efficiency reforms and distributed (off-grid) wind, solar, geo-thermal and kinetic (wave or water current) sources of energy remain as potential sources to be developed. Singapore has developed an energy efficiency program, with eco-label systems.[29] Thailand has a green-label scheme to promote resource conservation and sustainable development practices. Such programs address urban populations. The Philippines is encouraging the production and use of biofuels (biodiesel),

[28] M. Kummu, O. Varis and J. Sarkhula, "Impacts of Land Surface Changes on Regional Hydrology in Mainland Southeast Asia," in Lebel et al., *Critical States*.

[29] See www.e2singapore.gov.sg.

mostly from coconut oil.[30] Potential biodiesel feed stocks in the Philippines are jatropha and palm oil.

ASEAN's region-wide environmental profile appears in the annual *Environmental Performance Index* (EPI), prepared by Yale University. It focuses on measuring how nations reduce environmental stresses to human health (Environmental Health Objective) and protect ecosystems and natural resources (Ecosystem Vitality Objective).[31] ASEAN member states assessed in 2008 had scores of 53.8 to 84, compared with scores in all 149 nations of 39.1 to 95.5.[32] In the most recent EPI (2014), the scores ranged from 27.44 (Myanmar) to 81.78 (Singapore), contrasted with 15.47 (Somalia) to 87.67 (Switzerland) at the international level.[33] The relatively better performance of ASEAN member states compared to states in other regions can be considered one measure of the success of ASEAN intergovernmental collaboration. It may be posited that performance is better when regional integration is pursued than in regions where it is weaker.

How ASEAN addresses each of the five key themes identified here may provide a test for whether ASEAN legal integration is producing the salutary impacts intended by ASEAN.

[30] This is regulated by the Biofuels Act of 2006. See www.senate.gov.ph/republic_acts/ra%209367.pdf.

[31] See http://epi.yale.edu/epi/country-rankings.

[32] See 2008 *Environmental Performance Index* at ibid.

[33] See 2014 *Environmental Performance Index*, at ibid.

3.2.1 Biodiversity conservation and natural and cultural heritage

ASEAN intergovernmental cooperation on the protection of nature and parks is among its strongest and oldest themes. The ASEAN experts on the environment in 1978 defined the region's "Heritage Parks" and recommended that "these be given the highest regional recognition so that their importance as conservation areas would be appreciated internationally."[34] The ASEAN Group on Nature Conservation has developed criteria for the consistent selection, establishment and management of Heritage Parks in each ASEAN member state. On November 29, 1984, the Second ASEAN Ministerial Meeting in Bangkok issued its Declaration on Heritage Parks and Reserves.[35] This was replaced in 2003 by the ASEAN Declaration on Heritage Parks. Thirty-five such protected areas have been established as of April 2015.[36]. This record complements many national and regional parks and protected areas that are also established in ASEAN member states. The states have protected area agencies, such as national parks authorities, and most are members of the International

[34] First Meeting of ASEAN Experts Group on the Environment, Jakarta, December 18–20, 1978.

[35] ASEAN Declaration on Heritage Parks and Reserves, Bangkok, November 29, 1984. The Declaration can be found at www.aseansec.org/6078.htm.

[36] See http://chm.aseanbiodiversity.org/index.php?option=com_wrapper&view=wrapper&Itemid=110; and M. T. Uriarte, S. Bugna-Barrer and B. P. Botengan, *The ASEAN Heritage Parks: A Journey to the Nature Wonders of Southeast Asia* (ASEAN Centre for Biodiversity, 2010).

Union for the Conservation of Nature (IUCN) and participate in the World Commission on Protected Areas.

The ASEAN Declaration on Heritage Parks (2003) was prompted by concern with "the necessity to conserve national protected areas of the ASEAN member countries." It was preceded by an earlier Declaration in 1984 with the founding ASEAN member states. The 2003 Declaration is an excellent example of ASEAN integration, recognizing "that conservation areas should be managed to maintain ecological processes and life support systems, preserve genetic diversity; ensure sustainable utilization of species and ecosystems; and maintain wilderness that are of scenic, cultural, educational, research, recreational and tourism values." It states that a master plan should be drawn for each heritage park to include but not to be limited to management guidelines, research on the structure and function of ecosystems and education on wilderness values; noting that "environmental concerns transcend national boundaries and that individual states are primarily responsible for their respective identified heritage sites."

As at April 1, 2015, there are thirty-five ASEAN Heritage Parks (AHPs) established in the ten member states.[37] The criteria for qualifying as an ASEAN Heritage Park as outlined by ASEAN Senior Officials on the Environment in December 2003 are:

[37] Brunei has declared one Heritage Park; Cambodia two; Indonesia three; Lao PDR one; Malaysia three; Myanmar seven; the Philippines five; Singapore two; Thailand four and Vietnam five. An ASEAN Centre for Biodiversity has been established in Los Banos, Philippines. See *Asia Protected Planet Report 2014: Tracking Progress towards Targets for Protected Areas in Asia* (UNEP, 2014).

1. Ecological completeness – an intact ecological process and capacity to regenerate with minimal human intervention;
2. Representativeness – a variety of ecosystems or species typical of a particular region;
3. Naturalness – in natural condition, such as a second-growth forest or a rescued coral reef formation, with natural processes still occurring;
4. High conservation importance –global significance for the conservation of important or valuable species, ecosystems or genetic resources, evoking respect for nature when people see it, as well as a feeling of loss when its natural condition is lost;
5. Legally gazetted area – must be identified, defined and allocated by law or any legally accepted instrument of member states; and used primarily as a protected area with well-defined boundaries.

Loss of species in the ASEAN region is a cause for concern. Many species are endemic to specific islands, and logging and other land use changes are undertaken without an assessment of the rare flora and fauna in the same location. In addition, hunting, fragmentation of forest habitats and land conversions and degradation are also threats to ecosystems and their flora and fauna across most of the ASEAN region. ASEAN resources are not adequate to monitor or address those activities that damage biodiversity.[38] AHPs are of high conservation value and it is important that they be efficiently

[38] D. Murdiyarso, R. Lasco, D. Sheil, U. R. Wasrin, M. van Noordswijk and E. Meijaard, "Land Transformation and Its Consequences," in Lebel et al., *Critical States*, pp. 139–42.

managed and not be paper parks. While some are well managed, such as Singapore's Sungei Buloh Wetland Reserve, this cannot be said of all the AHPs.[39]

Building on the tradition of cooperation in protected areas, there is significant cooperation on biodiversity stewardship and protection of flora and fauna. The ASEAN member states cooperate through the Conference of the Parties for the United Nations Convention on Biological Diversity (CBD). All are members of the Convention on International Trade in Endangered Species of Wild Fauna and Flora (CITES), although enforcement of CITES remains problematic across the region for lack of monitoring and enforcement resources. Indonesia, Malaysia and the Philippines have joined South Pacific states to establish and apply the "Coral Triangle Initiative on Coral Reefs, Fisheries and Food Security" to protect endangered species in the coral reefs in the ASEAN region. The ASEAN environment ministers in 2002 adopted the ASEAN Criteria for Marine Heritage Areas, Criteria for National Marine Protected Areas and the Marine Water Quality Criteria for the ASEAN region.[40] In addition, the ASEAN Centre for Biodiversity, based in the Philippines,

39 Jamal M. Gavi, "It is high time that ASEAN countries stop finding excuses for failure to protect their parks. Synergy and collaboration between government and non-government actors and the ASEAN secretariat is required" (Gavi is a biodiversity conservation and governance specialist in the University of Indonesia). He presented a paper at the IUCN World Parks Congress, November 12–19, 2014, Sydney. See "Root out problems threatening ASEAN parks," *The Straits Times*, November 20, 2014.

40 Fourth ASEAN State of the Environment Report, 2009, pp. 47–8.

has organized four ASEAN Heritage Parks Conferences and developed collaborative programs among park managers in each member state. The ASEAN Heritage Parks are effectively a system harmonized region-wide to provide environmental stewardship for these natural areas that are important globally.

ASEAN's effective focus on protected areas has deflected from a focus on ecosystem services to the maintenance of ecosystems relevant to human needs, as reflected in the Millennium Ecosystem Assessment.[41] Nonetheless, the record of biodiversity cooperation has provided a sound foundation for ASEAN extending its collaborative work into the realm of ecosystem services. More than half of the world's ecosystems are degraded and ASEAN needs to prevent this trend from becoming worse in its region.

3.2.2 *Freshwater resources and forests*

The diverse forests of Southeast Asia frame the watersheds for the region's drinking water resources, biological diversity and agricultural activities. Despite the hydrologic links between forests and surface waters and aquifers, the environmental laws of the ASEAN region treat these two related natural resource sectors separately. Deforestation is an acute problem across the region, and its adverse impacts on flooding, soil erosion and sedimentation harm human life, settlements and infrastructure. ASEAN has the basic framework

[41] Millennium Ecosystem Assessment, *Ecosystems and Human Well-being: Biodiversity Synthesis* (World Resources Institute, 2005).

to address these challenges, but much remains to be done. Each area of cooperation can be surveyed to suggest what should be done.

Water resources

While water is abundant in the ASEAN region, its availability for human use is problematic. Because the region's countries vary in location and population, per capita use of water is high in certain states, such as Malaysia, Lao PDR and Brunei Darussalam. The availability of renewable water resources is highest in Indonesia (2,838 billion m^3), Myanmar (479 billion m^3) and Vietnam (366 billion m^3), while Thailand (210 billion m^3) and Cambodia (120 billion m^3) have lower volumes available. Singapore recycles water, harvests rainfall, has a desalinization plant and also imports water from Malaysia to supply its water needs (49 percent domestic, 51 percent industrial). In Indonesia, 59 percent of water use is for agriculture, while Thailand devotes 75 percent to agriculture. Vietnam uses 68 percent for agriculture and 24 percent for industry with only 8 percent allocated for domestic uses. With the exception of Singapore, management and conservation of water supply is not highly regulated, and best management practices are not yet a part of water resources law or administration.[42]

As populations grow, water use intensifies. Unless demand-side management and supply-side conservation measures are established, water demand across ASEAN is expected to double in the coming five decades. In urban

[42] Fourth ASEAN State of the Environment Report, 2009, p. 32.

areas, water pollution denies ready use of large volumes of water. Growing urbanization and industrialization contribute to increases in pollution. In Indonesia, twenty-seven out of thirty rivers evaluated in 2007 were found to be contaminated, and Jakarta's Citarum River was labelled the world's most contaminated river.[43] In Thailand, rivers classified as poor rose from 29 percent in 2005 to 48 percent in 2007.

Moreover, new demands are made on limited groundwater aquifers and lakes, and reservoirs. For example, water demand in Malaysia was 7,359 million liters per day in 2005; 15,285 million liters in 2010; and is estimated to be 20,338 million liters in 2020. Despite the lack of access to unpolluted waters near and in cities, ASEAN supplies potable water at levels that approximate to the world average. Measures to improve sanitation in Cambodia, Lao PDR, Myanmar and Vietnam have made demonstrable progress. Laws to enhance water quality management have been important. The Philippines has strengthened its legislation for water quality.[44]

The ASEAN Strategic Plan of Action on Water Resources Management, discussed in Chapter 5, represents an important region-wide response to the water challenges of states and localities across the region. Broader issues of hydrology will require action equal to the issues of water quality and supply for human use. Increased rainfall volumes

43 www.weather.com/news/news/worlds-most-polluted-rivers-20130627#/5.

44 Presidential Decree 856, Code on Sanitation of the Philippines; Presidential Decree 984, Pollution Control Law; and Republic Act 9725, Philippine Clean Water Act of 2004.

and intense typhoons cause massive flooding, resulting in damage to life and property and the contamination of drinking water supplies. The Philippines, Cambodia, Lao PDR, Vietnam and Thailand have endured massive disruptions due to floods. Both rural and urban drainage systems have been overwhelmed by recent extreme weather events. For example, in October 2011, after three typhoons inundated the region, more than 1.2 million people were displaced in Cambodia and 13 percent of the rice crop destroyed (100,000 hectares of rice fields destroyed); 17 of Cambodia's 23 provinces experienced damage to 3,000 km of roads and 160 bridges were submerged, with 1,100 schools and 100 hospitals destroyed. Vietnam experienced 1.2 million displaced persons and 300,000 hectares of farmland under water. Lao PDR had 430,000 persons displaced and 64,000 hectares of farmland inundated. Thailand had more than one million displaced people, and barely averted an inundation of all of Bangkok. Thirty of its seventy-seven provinces were inundated and 1.46 million hectares of land were under water. Industrial production was lost, disrupting supply chains in computer and electrical equipment globally.[45]

Wetlands are essential for the protection of upstream and downstream areas from flooding. ASEAN acknowledges the need to protect wetlands across the region, but the local authorities and nations have yet to deploy effective wetlands protection programs or projects to expand wetlands for flood control purposes.

[45] N. Ghosh, "Floods Exact Heavy Toll in Cambodia," *The Straits Times*, October 12, 2011, p. A22.

Forests

Forests represent a major resource for ASEAN, in particular, timber and non-timber products such as water flows. Yet, forests are threatened by illegal logging and unsustainable forest management due in part to demands from regional and international markets. The transboundary nature of forest product transactions is of regional and global concern, and demands joint actions. Several ASEAN instruments called for the eradication of unsustainable practices in the forest sector by 2010. ASEAN has taken steps toward achieving sustainable forest management in the regions such as implementation of the ASEAN Strategic Alliance on Sustainable Forest Management. Under the Alliance, ASEAN may undertake collaborative partnership with other regional processes such as the EU Forest Law Enforcement, Governance and Trade, Asia Forest Partnership (AFP) and the East Asia Forest Law Enforcement and Governance (FLEG) initiative.

The East Asia FLEG process was introduced in 2001 (Bali Declaration 2001) to serve as an umbrella coalition of governments, international institutions, civil society and private sectors. It aims to enhance concerted and coordinated actions to combat illegal logging and its associated trade while improving forest governance in timber producing and consuming countries.[46] The ASEAN Ministers

[46] Forest Law Enforcement and Governance, East Asia Ministerial Conference, Bali, Indonesia, September 11–13, 2001. The Ministerial Declaration can be found at www.illegal-logging.info/uploads/Bali_ministerial_declaration.pdf.

on Agriculture and Forestry, "deeply concerned by the adverse impacts on forest resources brought about by illegal logging and its associated trade," resolved in 2007 to, inter alia: strengthen forest law enforcement; enhance collaborative activities in timber certification, country diagnostics and experience sharing; and build a platform for synergistic partnership and cooperation.

At the 30th Meeting of the ASEAN Ministers on Agriculture and Forestry in 2008, the ministers endorsed the Work Plan for Strengthening Forest Law Enforcement and Governance (FLEG) in ASEAN[47] for the period 2008 to 2015. Earlier, at the 11th Meeting of the ASEAN Senior Officials on Forestry where the Work Plan was first introduced and agreed upon, the ASEAN Regional Knowledge Network on FLEG[48] (ARKN-FLEG) was created to promote the use of a regional knowledge network. The ARKN-FLEG serves to broaden ASEAN's base of knowledge in forestry and help implement the Work Plan. The terms of reference for the

[47] Proposed Work Plan for Strengthening Forest Law Enforcement and Governance in ASEAN 2008–2015, Kuala Lumpur, July 31 to August 1, 2008. The Work Plan can be found at http://cmsdata.iucn.org/downloads/appendix2_b_proposed_work_plan_for_strengthening_fleg_in_asean.pdf.

[48] The ARKN-FLEG was established to encourage the use of regional knowledge networks (expert pools) to better inform ASEAN decision-makers. It is composed of FLEG experts from leading research institutions in ASEAN and among the ASEAN Senior Officials on Forestry as network members as well as leading international experts as resource persons. See www.aseanforest-chm.org/asean-regional-knowledge-network-on-forest-law-enforcement-and-governance-fleg/.

ARKN-FLEG include building knowledge of FLEG issues in other parts of the world such as the European Union Forest Law Enforcement, Governance and Trade and the Asia Forest Partnership. To date, the World Bank's Forest Law Enforcement and Governance (FLEG) East Asia and Pacific program[49] provides technical expertise and financial aid toward biodiversity conservation and the sustainable management of natural resources to six ASEAN member states, namely: Cambodia, Lao PDR, Indonesia, the Philippines, Thailand and Vietnam.

3.2.3 *Fisheries and the marine environment*

The ASEAN region's marine environment constitutes a major resource of over-arching importance. In essence, the waters and coasts of the archipelagos and marine seas characterize ASEAN's region. The seas are the paths for coastal transport; interregional and international shipping and trade; a source of fish and other living resources of the oceans; and the access to the hydrocarbons and mineral resources of the seabed. The maps of ASEAN are characterized as much by water as by land. There are extant sea border disputes between ASEAN member states, such as Vietnam and the Philippines, with the People's Republic of China. There are straits for navigation under the terms of the UN Law of the Sea Convention for free navigation through the territorial seas and exclusive economic zones, for example through the waters of Malaysia, Indonesia, Singapore and the Philippines. The marine environment is a

[49] The World Bank, *Environment in East Asia and Pacific: Forest Law Enforcement and Governance*, www.worldbank.org/eapfleg.

prime concern of ASEAN member states and there are tensions stemming from illegal fishing. Despite complaints from its neighbors, Indonesia sank thirty-three of thirty-eight foreign vessels illegally fishing in its territorial waters between 2007 and 2012; thirty-two of these foreign ships were from Vietnam. The Indonesian navy now blows up the fishing boats, after confiscating the ships and arresting the crew.[50]

Notwithstanding its importance, the marine environment of ASEAN is not a separate featured theme in the Fourth ASEAN State of the Environment Report (it is combined with freshwater ecosystems). The fish harvest from the ASEAN region has grown from 17,000 metric tons in 2000 to 26,000 in 2007. The ASEAN State of the Environment report notes that overfishing is a major problem. The coral reefs support more than 1,300 reef-associated fish species. Coral is at risk, and there is no regional assurance that the growing exploitation of finfish is at sustained yield levels. It is likely that depletion of fish species will preclude continuous increases in harvest.

ASEAN summarizes threats to coastal and marine resources as follows: (a) land-based sources of pollution degrade marine water quality (red tides exist along the coasts of the Philippines and Sabah, Malaysia); (b) prawn culture and aquaculture activities along the coastline degrade the marine environment; (c) unplanned development of coastal

[50] S. Webb, "Now THAT's how you Deal with Poachers!" MailOnline, December 21, 2014 at www.dailymail.co.uk/news/article-2882538/Now-s-deal-poachers-Indonesian-navy-blows-illegal-foreign-fishing-vessels-spectacular-fashion-confiscating-ships-arresting-crew.html.

land uses, without the benefit of coastal zone management plans; (d) shipping and sea-based activities, including oil spills, sludge disposal, ballast water changes, and mining in coastal areas; and (e) off-shore oil and gas exploration and production. These environmental problems are all subject to environmental laws, at international and national levels, and yet the states in the ASEAN region do not have the capacity to implement the laws. The enormous extent of the ASEAN seacoasts explains this problem in part. It is a vast area to regulate. Moreover, the watersheds of rivers encompass a vast inland area, whose cascading waters eventually pollute the marine environment.[51]

Regionally, and through its member states, ASEAN has significant capacity to address issues of coastal and marine resources.

The Southeast Asian Fisheries Development Center (SEAFDEC) is an autonomous intergovernmental body established in 1967.[52] Its mandate is "to develop and manage the fisheries potential of the region by rational utilization of the resources for providing food security and safety to the people and alleviating poverty through transfer of new technologies, research and information dissemination activities." Though not an ASEAN initiative, SEAFDEC established links with ASEAN and is supported by ASEAN in the implementation of some of its activities, such as sustainable fisheries, to reduce disparities among countries in the region.

[51] ASEAN Fourth State of the Environment Report, 2009, p. 49.

[52] www.seafdec.org/index.php/about.

SEAFDEC comprises eleven member countries: the ten countries of ASEAN as well as Japan, which provides financial and technical support. The Center operates through its Secretariat located in Thailand and has four technical departments: the Training Department; the Marine Fisheries Research Department; the Aquaculture Department; and the Marine Fishery Resources Development and Management Department. The declaration of Exclusive Economic Zones (EEZs) in the region requires SEAFDEC to play a more active role in assisting member countries to develop and manage the marine fisheries in the waters within the extended jurisdiction of their respective EEZs. It acknowledges that this task needs to be tackled on a regional basis.

Examples of regional action on fisheries issues is illustrated by each of SEAFDEC's four technical departments. They demonstrate that regional cooperation is both valued and pursued, albeit not directly through the ASEAN Working Group. This may be because these technical departments predate the ASEAN Working Group on ASEAN Seas and the Marine Environment.

SEAFDEC's Training Division (TD)

Established in Thailand in 1968, TD seeks to develop modern fishery techniques to aid regional fisheries with a more sustainable approach through the promotion of responsible fishing technologies and practices, exploration of resources and advancing the coastal fisheries management approach. Under the new Strategic Plan which was endorsed in 2006, the structure and activities of TD have been adjusted to emphasize the promotion of coastal fisheries management to ensure responsible resource utilization and sustainable livelihoods in coastal communities, and the promotion of offshore fisheries through the development of best fishing practices and energy optimization technology to ensure a stable supply of fish and reduce fishing pressure in coastal areas.

Marine Fisheries Research Department (MFRD)

Another illustration of building regional sustainable fishing practices is found in SEAFDEC's Marine Fisheries Research Department (MFRD). The MFRD was established in 1969 and is responsible for promoting, undertaking and coordinating research in fisheries' post-harvest technology and furthering the development of the fish processing industry in the region. Its task includes research and development on fisheries' post-harvest technology and practices, such as fish processing technology to optimize the utilization of harvested fish and enhance the quality and safety of fish and fishery products. MFRD also develops technology-based analytical methods to assess seafood safety and quality, and publishes several manuals as reference materials for the member countries.

Aquaculture Department

SEAFDEC's Aquaculture Department (AQD)[53] was established in the Philippines in 1973. AQD has been carrying out

[53] www.seafdec.org.ph/.

research, technology verification, training and information dissemination on a wide range of aquaculture disciplines, including broodstock management and seed quality improvement, promotion of responsible and environment-friendly aquaculture, diagnosis and control of aquatic diseases, aquaculture for stock enhancement, and culture of aquatic species under international concerns. The aquaculture commodities covered by AQD include fish, shrimps, mud crabs, mollusks and seaweeds. In addition, AQD also promotes good aquaculture practices and effective management of aquatic resources to support rural development and alleviate poverty.

Marine Fishery Resources Development and Management Department (MFRDMD)

Finally, SEAFDEC's Marine Fishery Resources Development and Management Department (MFRDMD)[54] was established in Malaysia (Kuala Teregganu) in 1992 to conduct activities on marine fishery resources focusing on biological studies of commercially-important fish species, resource assessment and management, and conservation and management of aquatic species of international concern, such as sharks and marine turtles. MFRDMD also implements activities that support the member countries in gathering information on inland capture fisheries, and developing indicators to be used for the sustainable development and management of fisheries.

[54] www.seafdec.org.my/v13/index.php?option=com_content&view=article&id=143&Itemid=4.

Notwithstanding the work undertaken through SEAFDEC, effective management of coastal fisheries that straddle national and international borders continues to be a challenge for ASEAN. Diminishing coastal fish stocks is the result of (a) national fisheries policies that address fishing primarily in national and coastal waters and not migratory fish nor those straddling borders; (b) management and administration that tend to focus on local waters and not on ASEAN-wide patterns; (c) demersal fish that are associated with different specific habitats during their life cycle, and conservation laws or policies do not cover the range of the species across its life cycles; and (d) human and material resources that enforce fishery laws are severely limited and the patrol area is vast, enabling unlawful practices to persist.[55]

ASEAN itself concludes in the Fourth State of the Environment Report that the slow progress in managing the coastal and marine environments is due to several factors: "lack of irrefutable and clear information about the nature and extent of the proven affecting the coastal and marine environment; legal and institutional complexities; non-involvement of local communities; weak multi-sectoral approaches," including inadequate use of financial incentives, reporting and environmental management systems, weak environmental impact assessment systems and incomplete legal instruments.[56] While these reasons may be sound, they at a minimum explain why ASEAN action on marine and

[55] M. C. Ablan-Lagman, "Managing Beyond Boundaries: Coastal Fisheries," in Lebel et al., *Critical States*, p. 329.

[56] ASEAN Fourth State of the Environment Report, 2009, p. 49.

coastal issues has made slow progress, but do not explain why the coastal and marine environment has not been accorded higher priority. ASEAN needs to build new modalities for linking its policy and law development to capacity-building efforts, such as those of SEAFDEC. Regional integration is not undertaken only by ASEAN, but ASEAN has the mandate to begin integrating policy that leads to a common set of legal norms. The shared marine environment of the region urgently needs strong ASEAN engagement – especially regarding fish harvests. Fisheries management cuts across economic, political and environmental sectors of ASEAN cooperation. Until the ASEAN ministerial meeting raises the sustainability of the marine environment to the ASEAN meeting of Heads of State, it is likely that coast, marine and fisheries issues will be characterized by unsustainable practices for some time to come.

The marine environment defines the ASEAN region in many ways. The ASEAN environmental cooperation programs are still at their early stages of exploring how to protect the coastal and marine environment. Lack of capacity is the primary reason for the apparent relegation of this sector to a lower priority than it warrants in light of its importance.

3.2.4 *Human settlements*

The people of the ASEAN member states experience the environment where they live. The region is characterized by a tradition of human settlements that have grown up over time, often for centuries. There is a shortage of capacity for spatial planning or laws for town and country development, efficient mass transportation, adequate housing and urban infrastructure generally. Many human settlements are along the coast, and planning will be needed to move coastal infrastructure to higher ground as sea levels rise. This is an opportunity for ASEAN to make urban redevelopment a high priority and build cooperation regionally. Similarly, people living in inland and rural areas deserve to have education and healthcare facilities, transport and other infrastructure. These are core elements of sustainable development. Some of the elements that ASEAN currently addresses for urban and rural populations illustrate what more will be needed.

Cities/urban habitats

The urban environment is a high priority for ASEAN's environmental focus. ASEAN's programs in health, transport and other sectors also focus on the cities. A city such as Singapore is already a global center for trade, finance, health and education. Singapore's growth has been carefully managed, with laws and administration well aligned.[57] Other cities, such as Manila, however, have grown rapidly and without comparable legal or planning systems. The Philippines enacted Metro Manila legislation to provide a planning and management regime for Metro Manila, but it is difficult, after the fact, to contain and reform incremental growth patterns, and Metro Manila with 2.5 million people living in slums is the largest gathering of squatter settlements in the Philippines. Throughout ASEAN's cities (with the exception

[57] See L.-H. Lye, "A Fine City in a Garden – A Study of Environmental Governance in Singapore," *SING. J. Legal Studies* (July 31, 2008) 68–117 at pp. 108–17.

of Singapore), providing housing has not kept pace with immigration. This in turn produces large volumes of refuse, and as landfills become scarce, cities are incinerating refuse, causing air pollution. Formal and informal recovery and recycling and reuse systems also emerge. Scavengers and junk buyers in the cities recover materials, and in Lao PDR and Cambodia recovered waste is exported to Vietnam for reprocessing.[58] Potable water and sanitary waste treatment are insufficient in most of the cities in the ASEAN region. Unsanitary landfills contaminate groundwater supplies.

Urban environmental issues are of concern because most of ASEAN's governance takes place in and through cities. The growth of cities through immigration is projected to absorb the bulk of the overall population growth. Urban concentrations are estimated to double in size by 2025. These human habitats will be the largest their nations have ever experienced, and will tax the capacity of ASEAN's cooperative institutions to share city planning, transport, jobs, health, education and other sectoral management experiences. For the first time in Southeast Asia, the vast majority of the population will be urban and not rural.

The environmental infrastructure demands for cities are significant. Most ASEAN cities already experience shortages of potable water supplies, and lack facilities for the treatment and recycling of wastewater. There are also inadequacies in public housing, parks and recreation spaces, electricity supplies, air quality control systems, and solid and

[58] K. S. Yap and L. Lebel, "Incomplete Urbanization," in Lebel et al., *Critical States*.

hazardous waste management regimes. Government budgets allocate very little funding to municipal environmental services; new environmental needs audits will be required, and the revenues and user fees allocated to meet the costs of establishing and sustaining urban environmental services. ASEAN cities will need to establish urban ecology programs and adequate planning regimes.[59] As cities industrialize and create jobs, they will also need to establish better environmental management practices. Many Asian cities have ISO 9000 and ISO 14000 environmental quality management and audit systems, but they tend to be isolated by factory, company or industrial sectors. ASEAN environmental agencies will need to apply city-wide environmental management systems to cope with the challenges that they face now and in the near future. Regionally, Singapore offers a successful model of phased urban development that has been emulated in new urban developments in parts of China, but not yet in Southeast Asia, where there exists a mix of ASEAN sensitivities, such as not wishing to appear to make comparisons that advantage one sovereign state over another, and a sense that urban settlements are quintessentially a domestic and local issue not appropriate for a regional intergovernmental collaboration. Without cooperation on urban growth, however, current patterns of urban growth suggest that neither the environment nor the economies of the region are likely to sustain a high quality of life.

[59] See, for example, M. Chertow, E. S. Choi and K. Lee, "The Material Consumption of Singapore's Economy: An Industrial Ecology Approach," in Savage and Lye, *Environment and Climate Change in Asia*.

As one study reports:

> Urban centers are expanding … in 1950 neither Jakarta, Manila or Bangkok were among the top thirty most populous cities in the world, but by 2000 Jakarta ranked 12th, Manila 17th and Bangkok 27th … remote sensing shows that commercial areas in the Bangkok metropolitan region grew by 14 per cent between 1988 and 1994. Land cover dynamics in Bangkok follow a trend of conversion from agriculture to open land, open land to residential, and residential to commercial.[60]

This pattern is common to most growth in urban settlements across ASEAN. The growth of cities drives the loss of land for agriculture and forests.

Human habitats are, in fact, a primary environmental concern across each of the ASEAN member states. The cities in ASEAN depend on ecosystems around and within their urban developments for many ecosystem services and indeed for their very survival, and yet no municipal, national or ASEAN-wide matrix takes account of the economic value of ecosystems to cities.[61] As a matter of comparative national law and also ASEAN regional policy and cooperation, the pace of development of ASEAN institutional capacity for urban environmental stewardship lags behind the rapidly growing scale of needs in human habitats. It should be noted

[60] J. H. Samek, D. L. Skole, D. X. Lan, I. Gunawan, A. Karsidi, S. Mastura, S. A. S. Thongmanivong and H. Sanjaya, "Land Cover Dynamics," in Lebel et al., *Critical States*, p. 147.

[61] See J. Thampapillai, "The Economic Valuation of Urban Ecosystem Services," in Savage and Lye, Environment and Climate Change in Asia.

that this phenomenon is not unique to ASEAN but is global. The worldwide United Nations Habitat Programme is a very modest and wholly unfunded exercise. States leave cities to fend for themselves. What fails globally may succeed regionally if the ASEAN legal and policy regimes can be aligned to assist cities to help themselves and their urban populations.

Countryside/rural habitats

As opposed to urban habitats, rural populations across ASEAN are found along most of its coasts, mountains and rural landscape. Much of ASEAN has rich terrestrial resources, and 43 percent of its land remains forested. Nonetheless, the rate of deforestation has been high in some nations such as the Philippines where the percentage of forest is 26.5 percent, or Thailand (28.9 percent), or Vietnam (33.2 percent). Malaysia, Cambodia, Brunei Darussalam and Myanmar have forest cover greater than 50 percent.[62] The ASEAN region holds 60 percent of the world's peatlands (25 million hectares), which sequester large volumes of greenhouse gases; conversion of peat wetlands to agriculture, primarily in Indonesia, permits potentially large amounts of these gases to enter the atmosphere, contributing significantly to the global warming phenomenon. ASEAN has adopted a Peatlands Policy to focus on this concern.[63] Along the coast, ASEAN hosts important mangrove forests.

62 ASEAN Fourth State of the Environment Report, 2009, p. 54.

63 2006 ASEAN Peatland Management Strategy, Cebu, the Philippines, November 10, 2006. The management strategy can be found at http://haze.asean.org/asean-peatland-management-strategy-apms/.

Mangroves are critical resources for marine fish life cycles, and protect upland areas from storm surges. Despite these benefits they bring to the ecosystem, across ASEAN mangroves declined from 6,385,040 hectares in 1980 to 5,240,830 in 2005.[64]

Land management systems in many member states do not yet make provisions to plan to maintain large well-connected forest landscapes that are essential for biodiversity, wildlife corridors and watersheds. Forest management will be an essential component of sustaining ecosystems and biodiversity in ASEAN.

ASEAN member states are traditionally agriculturally based societies, and the agricultural land uses are traditional. Farmlands remain to be mapped in many places, and spatial land use planning is not yet practiced. Conversions of forest to farmland, or to plantations for commercial palm oil or other crops, continue. Few programs exist to promote and educate on best management practices for farming. Where farmlands are near urban settlements, they tend toward conversion to non-farm uses, and this puts pressure on more remote farmlands to produce and ship goods to urban settlements. Moreover, soil fertility in the region has declined in 56 million hectares, of which 26 million hectares are in Thailand alone. Dependency on nitrogen fertilizers and pesticides is on the rise in the region's agricultural lands.[65]

[64] Fourth ASEAN State of the Environment Report, 2009, p. 32.

[65] P. Thongbai, "Agricultural Expansion and Intensification," in Lebel et al., *Critical States*, pp. 168–9.

Both agriculture and forestry play essential roles in the livelihoods of the people of the ASEAN region. Many of the poorest individuals subsist on rural farms, and if poverty alleviation is to be an ASEAN priority, as well as being advanced as key to meeting the United Nations Sustainable Development Goals, then the environmental practices of lands and forests need to be given higher priority focus.

3.2.5 *Atmosphere*

Air quality is important to the health of residents in urban settlements. Long-distance transportation of air pollutants is a regional, interstate problem, and also contributes to global phenomena such as "acid rain" or atmospheric brown cloud and global warming, as discussed in Chapter 4 of this study. Air pollution stems from industrialization, use of motor vehicles and uncontrolled land and forest fires.

ASEAN treats air quality as essentially a priority for its urban human settlements and ASEAN member states monitor air pollution in their cities.[66] Major cities regularly report a number of days with air quality unsafe to breathe. The ASEAN member states are gradually adopting the standards for petrol and diesel vehicles used in the USA[67] and the EU.[68] However, there is a practice of selling used cars without

[66] See Table 6.5 detailing the pollution monitoring and control rules and practices in the ASEAN member states in Chapter 6, "Atmosphere," in the Fourth ASEAN State of the Environment Report, 2009, pp. 73–4.

[67] The Clean Air Act (CAA) 42 U.S.C. 7401-7671q. (1970).

[68] European Commission [EC] Directive 96/69/EC.

emission controls from more affluent ASEAN member states to less affluent states – not unlike similar practices in Europe or North America – and this slows the implementation of air quality enhancements across the ASEAN region. Obsolete automotive air quality systems are perpetuated. The lack of adequate mass transportation systems compounds this problem. ASEAN recognizes the need to cooperate on techniques to improve urban air quality, but the growth of urban settlements exceeds the administration of much-needed air quality control systems.

With respect to long-distance air pollution, ASEAN's Roadmap for an ASEAN Community 2009–2015 states as an objective to: "prevent transboundary haze pollution as a result of land and/or forest fires through concerted national efforts and intensified regional action and international cooperation", pursued in accordance with the provisions of the 2003 ASEAN Agreement on Transboundary Haze Pollution. Little progress has been made toward this goal, as Indonesia, the main source of forest fires in the region, chose not to ratify this agreement until late 2014. ASEAN has yet to take firm steps to create regional collaborative capacity to control and extinguish forest fires, and to enforce laws that prevent clearing forests by burning.[69] Air pollution from ASEAN member states contributes to atmospheric brown

[69] Proposals for this sort of regional cooperation, based on practices in North America and Europe, are well understood, but not yet adopted. See N. A. Robinson, "Forest Fires as a Common International Concern: Precedents for The Progressive Development of International Environmental Law," *Pace Envir'l L. Rev.* 18(2)(2001) 459.

cloud, but neither international public law[70] nor ASEAN policy and law addresses this phenomenon. Similarly, ASEAN does not recognize the contribution that air pollution makes to the contamination of coastal marine and ocean waters.

However, a new phase began in September 2014 when Singapore passed its Transboundary Haze Pollution Act.[71] The Act seeks to impose criminal and civil penalties upon entities that do business in Singapore and are responsible for land clearance fires that occur outside Singapore's territorial boundaries but cause air pollution within Singapore. The finding of civil liability or criminal responsibility is facilitated by a number of presumptions in the Act that help to establish a causal connection to enable the entity to be charged. Shortly after the enactment of this law and after new elections in Indonesia, the Indonesian Parliament announced its ratification of the Haze Agreement. Indonesia's ratification of the ASEAN Haze Agreement lays the foundation for cooperative enforcement measures to prevent new forest fires and facilitate a more robust regional collaboration toward a resolution.

In each of the five aspects of environmental and developmental issues set forth above, both ASEAN collectively and its individual member states are engaged in efforts to establish sustainable development patterns. The problem

[70] United Nations Economic Commission for Europe, *The 1979 Geneva Convention on Long Distance Transboundary Air Pollution,* (Geneva, 1979). The Convention applies in East and West Europe and no comparable regime applies to the Asian or Southeast Asian region.

[71] Singapore's laws can be accessed at http://statutes.agc.gov.sg/aol/home.w3p.

is that they are too modest, too peripheral to core governmental decision-making, and too incremental to be having an impact in abating or reversing unsustainable patterns of environmental degradation. Often the environmental legislation may be sound, but the compliance and enforcement systems are lacking. They are not undertaken at a scale commensurate with the need, either nationally or regionally.

ASEAN policies and programs are not functioning at the regional scale required for them to be effective. The regional environmental trends overall are not positive. Scientific reports on environmental trends across the ASEAN region show a gradual loss of biological diversity, a reduction in ecosystems services when population growth in the region is on the rise and requires these services all the more, and a shift away from sustainable natural environmental management systems needed to sustain quality of life in cities.

ASEAN's Secretariat and its working groups are aware of these environmental degradation challenges and strive to address a number of them, but still its programs lag behind the trends in environmental degradation. ASEAN needs the means to elevate these issues to the level of ministers and heads of state, with action plans prepared for implementation. Until each environmental threat to sustainable development is addressed by a bespoke action plan, the desired levels of sustainable development will be unattainable. The disruptions resulting from environmental degradation, exacerbated by the effects of climate change, will undermine efforts at legal integration in ASEAN.

Yet, if ASEAN did not exist, regional cooperation to tackle such challenges would have to be invented. Much has been accomplished in building confidence across Southeast Asia and in the capacity to take collective action. Environmental decision-making has allowed ASEAN to scale up its efforts and embrace increasingly strong programs for capacity building and harmonization of environmental management standards and systems. This regional integration can be studied also through analysis of the environmental laws in each of the ASEAN member states. Having examined the five themes outlined above, we now have a baseline for comparing the strengths and weaknesses of ASEAN member states' environmental laws.

Chapter 4

Environmental sustainability laws in the ASEAN member states

A review of the national environmental legislation in each ASEAN member state illustrates that ASEAN displays both centrifugal and disparate tendencies in legal integration. ASEAN cooperation seeks harmonization and integration to facilitate steps toward region-wide environmental sustainability. However, individual states are driven by their historical and developmental legacies; priorities for ASEAN's sustainability are not always the same for national leaders. Most have not attained the recommended actions described in Agenda 21 to be considered sustainable societies, much less a model for sustainable development. Because of limitations in development state economies, problems with corruption and insufficient expertise, among other challenges, it may be unrealistic to assess legal integration in ASEAN solely from a classical model of international law. Conversely, if ASEAN member states chose to do so, the international environmental law agreements to which they are members provide them with many cooperative tools and legal frameworks for resolving environmental problems and attaining sustainable development.[1] ASEAN could collaborate with its member states to avail themselves of such opportunities.

[1] See N. A. Robinson, "Legal Redress of Transboundary Air Pollution Through Environmental Cooperation," in S. Jayakumar, T. Koh, R. Beckman and Hao Duy Phan (eds.), *Transboundary*

As sovereign states, international law regards each as equal, but as geographic countries, each has unique ecological challenges that differ substantially from state to state. Hence, national and sub-national environmental laws, and implementation of those laws, can be expected to vary greatly. Like all nations, the ASEAN member states may have enacted comparable bodies of environmental legislation through national law, and each may be a member of the various international treaties and multinational environmental agreements, but their capacity to implement treaty obligations also varies greatly. This reality is illustrated by a selective survey of some of the environmental legal issues in different ASEAN member states.

4.1 Southeast Asian legal systems and constitutions

With the establishment of colonies and protectorates in the region by Great Britain during the late eighteenth and nineteenth centuries, Brunei, Malaysia, Myanmar and Singapore came to inherit common law from the British legal system during their colonial rule. From their French colonial rule, the Indochinese countries (Vietnam, Lao PDR and Cambodia) acceded to a civil law system, though administered with socialist law since gaining their independence. Indonesia practices a civil law system based on a Roman-Dutch model influenced by customary (adat) law, while the legal system

Pollution – Evolving Issues of International Law and Policy (Edward Elgar, 2015), p. 362.

in the Philippines is a blend of civil law and common law from its Spanish and American rule, though common law is dominant. Thailand has been a constitutional monarchy since 1932; it is a civil law country with strong common law influences. It is also the only Southeast Asian country to have never been taken over by a foreign power or fallen to Japanese occupation.

As a reflection of the uneven integration toward environmental sustainability in the region, constitutional protection for the environment is present in only several ASEAN member states, namely: Cambodia, Indonesia, Myanmar, the Philippines, Thailand and Vietnam.

In Cambodia, protection of the environment and natural resources is delegated to the state,[2] which has broad powers to "establish a precise plan of management of land, water, air, wind, geology, ecological system, mines, energy, petrol and gas, rocks and sand, gems, forests and forestry products, wildlife, fish and aquatic resources."[3] While the first Constitution of Indonesia passed in 1945 had only one provision that referenced the environment subject to a citizen-primacy rule,[4] the Constitution[5] as amended in 2002 now contains two important provisions for environmental

[2] The Constitution of the Kingdom of Cambodia 1993, Chapter V, Article 59.

[3] Ibid.

[4] The 1945 Constitution of the Republic of Indonesia, Chapter XIV, Article 33(3).

[5] The 1945 Constitution of the Republic of Indonesia, as amended by the First Amendment of 1999, the Second amendment of 2000, the Third Amendment of 2001 and the Fourth Amendment of 2002.

protection: Article 33(4) seeks to integrate economic development with sustainability, and Article 28H(1) recognizes the right to a "good and healthy environment." While the ambit and meaning of these provisions have not been tested in court, they are often referred to in environmental laws and policies. The 2008 Constitution of Myanmar, which took effect from January 31, 2011, provides that the government "shall protect and conserve the natural environment."[6] The Constitution delegates power to the national legislature to enact laws toward environmental protection and restoration,[7] and to state and division legislatures to regulate environmental protection.[8] In addition, every citizen has the duty to "assist" the government in carrying out environmental conservation.[9]

The Philippines has led the region in passing innovative environmental legislation, for example the Supreme Court's rules for the writ of continuing mandamus and the writ of Kalikasan (nature). The 1987 Constitution of Philippines provides a strong legal basis for the protection of procedural and substantive human rights in relation to their environment. The Constitution mandates the state to "protect and advance the right of people to a balanced and healthful ecology in accord with the rhythm and harmony of nature."[10] Citizens are guaranteed access to information

[6] Constitution of the Republic Union of Myanmar (2008), Chapter 1, Section 45.

[7] Ibid., at Chapter 4, Section 96.

[8] Ibid., at Chapter 4, Section 196.

[9] Ibid., at Chapter 8, Section 290..

[10] 1987 Constitution of the Republic of the Philippines Article II, Section 16.

"on matters of public concern,"[11] as well as the right to participate in the decision-making process.[12] This procedural right is supplemented by the state's adoption and implementation of a full public disclosure policy.[13] In addition, the Constitution established the Office of Ombudsman as "protectors of people"[14] against misconduct and abuses by government officials and public civil servants. In 2012, the Environmental Ombudsman's office was reactivated, and a team of twenty-six attorneys has been appointed to "handle all cases involving violations of environmental laws or concerning environmental protection that will be filed with the office."[15]

While there have always been statutes governing natural resources and the environment in Thailand, conservation principles had never been systematically incorporated into law until the promulgation of the Constitution of the Kingdom of Thailand B.E. 2517 (1974). The present Constitution B.E. 2540 (1997) continues to embody principles of environmental conservation by seeking sustainable management and usage of natural resources and the environment;[16] requiring environmental impact assessments for development projects and activities;[17] and designating the

11 Ibid., at Article III, Section 7.

12 Ibid., at Article XIII, Section 16.

13 Ibid., at Article II, Section 28.

14 Ibid., at Article XI, Section 12.

15 See Office of the Ombudsman, www.ombudsman.gov.ph/index.php?home=1&pressId=Mjgw.

16 Constitution of the Kingdom of Thailand B.E. 2550 (2007) Chapter III, Part 12, Article 66.

17 Ibid., at Chapter III, Part 12, Article 67.

state with the authority to implement land, natural resources and environment policies.[18] Like its Southeast Asian counterparts, the Constitution imposes a duty on citizens to conserve natural resources and guarantees their right to a healthful and decent environment;[19] public participation;[20] access to information;[21] and the right to sue governmental agencies.[22] As for Vietnam, the Constitution provides that "The land, forests, rivers and lakes, water sources, underground natural resources, resources in the territorial waters, on the continental shelf and in the air space ... belonging to the State are owned by the people."[23] Article 29 states "All State offices, armed forces units, economic establishments, social organisations and every citizen have to observe State regulations on the appropriate utilisation of natural resources and on environmental protection. All acts resulting in depletion and destruction of the environment are strictly prohibited."

At a local level, ASEAN member states have promulgated legislation directed at conservation and protection of the environment. These include: Law on Environmental Protection and Management of Natural Resources Act 1996 (Cambodia); Environmental Management Act 1982, 1997 and 2009 (Indonesia); Law on Environmental Protection 1999 (Lao PDR); Environmental Quality Act 1974 (Malaysia); Environmental

18 Ibid., at Chapter V, Part 8, Article 85.

19 Ibid., at Chapter III, Part 10, Article 57.

20 Ibid., at Article 58.

21 Ibid., at Article 56.

22 Ibid., at Article 60.

23 1992 Constitution of the Socialist Republic of Viet Nam (amended 2001), Chapter II, Article 17.

Protection and Management Act 1999 (Singapore); National Environmental Quality Act 1992 (Thailand); and Environmental Protection Law 2005 (Viet Nam). In particular, some of these laws (e.g. those of Indonesia, Philippines and Thailand) contain principles established in Agenda 21 and the Rio Declaration on Environment and Development, namely: the polluter-pays principle[24], the right to public participation[25] and environmental impact assessments.[26]

Notwithstanding that these principles are not incorporated by more ASEAN member states through legislation, member states do implement these principles as part of their environmental management plans. In accordance with the polluter-pays and environmental taxation principles, Singapore has implemented an electronic road payment system since 1998 to regulate road usage and traffic conditions, and imposes hefty taxes on cars, as well as an innovative Certificate of Entitlement program to limit ownership and discourage the use of motorized vehicles.[27]

Having recently emerged from a strict socialist regime, the Indochinese states are only now seeking modernization. Hence, the laws drafted are not as comprehensive and sometimes leave considerable gaps, particularly

[24] Principle 16, The Rio Declaration on Environment and Development.

[25] Ibid., Principle 25.

[26] Ibid., Principle 17.

[27] See L.-H. Lye, "Environmental Taxation in the Management of Traffic in Singapore," in L.-H. Lye, J. Milne, H. Ashiabor, K. Deketelaere and L. Kreiser (eds.), *Critical Issues in Environmental Taxation*, Vol. VII (Oxford University Press, 2007), pp. 205–25.

where institutional responsibility is involved. In contrast, the Philippines, Indonesia and Thailand have a strong presence of non-governmental organizations (NGOs) and environmental lawyers who are unafraid to clamor for change or bring legal suits to challenge the interpretation or implementation of environmental laws.

4.2 Regional and international cooperation

A number of statutes, regulations and other legal instruments for environmental management have been stimulated in each ASEAN member state through regional ASEAN cooperation. It should be noted that these instruments are fine examples of integration at an ASEAN level; not only are these instruments crafted after discussions among ASEAN ministers, they indicate consensus among different member states on the policies and provisions espoused in these instruments. Some of these instruments remain to be implemented, such as the ASEAN Agreement on Transboundary Haze Pollution, while others have advanced significantly, such as the ASEAN Declaration on Heritage Parks. Apart from the multilateral environmental agreements (MEAs) and relatively few ASEAN "hard law" instruments, there are many environmental "soft law" policies and programs in the ASEAN region that are well implemented and observed. These include: establishment of the ASEAN Centre for Biodiversity (ACB) in Los Baños, Philippines; creation of ASEAN's Wildlife Enforcement Network (ASEAN-WEN) in Thailand; and promulgation of the Memorandum of

Understanding on ASEAN Sea Turtle Conservation,[28] with Malaysia designated as the coordinator.

ASEAN member states have demonstrated full commitment to major MEAs with 100 percent ratification while the more recent MEAs have achieved high rates of ratification.[29] To date, all member states are parties to the Convention on Biological Diversity (CBD); Convention on International Trade in Endangered Species of Wild Flora and Fauna (CITES); United Nations Convention on Law of the Sea (UNCLOS); Vienna Convention for the Protection of the Ozone Layer and the Montreal Protocol on Substances that Deplete the Ozone Layer; United Nations Framework Convention on Climate Change (UNFCCC) and the Kyoto Protocol; Stockholm Convention on Persistent Organic Pollutants (POPs), and the UNESCO World Heritage Convention. With the exception of Myanmar, all states are parties to the Basel Convention on the Control of Transboundary Movement of Hazardous Wastes and their Disposal. Eight member states (excluding Brunei and Singapore) are parties to the Convention on Wetlands of International Importance especially as Waterfowl Habitat.[30] All states excluding Singapore are parties to the Convention to Combat Desertification, but only six states are parties to

[28] Memorandum of Understanding on ASEAN Sea Turtle Conservation and Protection, Bangkok, September 12, 1997, www.aseansec.org/6185.htm.

[29] Fourth State of the Environment Report, 2009, p. 103.

[30] Cambodia has designated three sites, Indonesia has six sites, Lao PDR two, Malaysia six, Myanmar one, the Philippines four, Thailand eleven and Vietnam has four sites.

the Rotterdam Convention on Prior Informed Consent.[31] Presently, the Philippines is the only party to the Bonn Convention on Migratory Species.

Implementation of the MEAs, however, has been uneven at best. While the Philippines, Singapore, Malaysia, Indonesia and Thailand have competent environmental laws, enforcement is generally weak in these member states with the exception of Singapore and Malaysia.

4.3 Protection and conservation of biological, natural and cultural heritage

4.3.1 Biological diversity: Flora and fauna

The ASEAN Agreement on the Conservation of Nature and Natural Resources was the first ASEAN agreement on the environment. Endorsed by the then six ASEAN member states[32] in 1985, the Agreement was crafted by legal experts from the International Union for Conservation of Nature's Commission on Environmental Law in consultation with regional environmental agencies. While the Agreement was far sighted and comprehensive, its obligations were advanced and beyond the provisions of most of the environmental law of the states in the region. ASEAN member states

[31] These are Indonesia, Malaysia, the Philippines, Singapore, Thailand and Vietnam.

[32] Brunei, Malaysia, Indonesia, the Philippines, Singapore and Thailand are parties to the Agreement on the Conservation of Nature and Natural Resources, signed on July 9, 1985, in Kuala Lumpur, Malaysia. However, only Indonesia, the Philippines and Thailand have ratified.

are reluctant to agree to hard law obligations that they are not yet ready to observe. In this respect, Southeast Asia is different from Africa, where a comparable regional agreement has been ratified and in force for some time, with progressive steps to obtain compliance and enforcement of its measures. Today, this Agreement is ratified by only three of the ten ASEAN member states and is not yet in force. Prospectively, it could provide ASEAN with a useful framework for the regional integration of environmental laws.

Poaching of wildlife and trade in endangered species continue to be a major concern in all ASEAN member states despite the presence of national laws that implement CITES. Millions of wild birds and reptiles, highly endangered turtles and pangolins are exported yearly. The widespread loss of pangolins due largely to demands for its meat, scales and traditional medicinal value in Vietnam and China has led experts to believe they may be on the verge of extinction in the region.[33] In recent years, captive breeding has become another means of illegal trade. Wildlife is often fraudulently declared as captive bred, therein providing a market for wild-caught species. The monitoring of captive-breeding facilities is weak across all member states, which generally lack manpower, training, funding and resources.[34]

33 B. Block, "Illegal Pangolin Trade Threatens Rare Species," Worldwatch Institute: Eye on Earth, www.worldwatch.org/node/6198; see also A. Nayar, "Wildlife Trade Threatens Southeast Asia's Rare Species," *Nature*, December 22, 2009, www.nature.com/news/2009/091220/full/news.2009.1136.html.

34 V. Nijman and C. Shepherd, *Wildlife Trade from ASEAN to the EU: Issues with the Trade in Captive-bred Reptiles from Indonesia* (TRAFFIC International, 2009).

Declaring a nature reserve is often not enough to ensure the safety of its inhabitants.[35] A recent review[36] of wildlife trade policy in Vietnam concluded that the present policy has a heavy focus on the protection of wildlife and law enforcement, but "development of legal utilization is not given equal attention."[37] The review draws on the notion that community rights to harvest and trade should be acknowledged, for livelihoods that rely heavily on exploitation of natural resources are severely affected by a blanket ban on such use and trade. Little funding has been made available for wildlife rescue.[38] The implementation of a wildlife trade policy has been ineffectual in part because goals are too ambitious and there is a lack of monitoring and evaluation capacity.[39] Recommendations include increasing the number of highly trained and well-equipped enforcement staff at all points along the trade chain, using more sniffer dogs, conducting DNA tests to search for wildlife products, and employing smart-phone applications with species identification programs.

ASEAN-WEN[40] is one of the largest wildlife law enforcement networks in the world, and it involves

[35] See Wildlife Conservation Society at www.wcs.org/where-we-work/asia/indonesia.aspx.

[36] M. Nguyen, V. Du, V. Nguyen, V. Hoang, H. Nguyen, N. Pham, T. Than and C. Doan, Report on the Review of Vietnam's Wildlife Trade Policy, CRES/FPD/UNEP/CITESIUED, Hanoi, Vietnam (2007), at www.cites.org/common/prog/policy/Vietnam_wildlife_trade_policy_review.pdf.

[37] Ibid., at p. 61.

[38] Ibid., at p. 62.

[39] Ibid.

[40] See www.asean-wen.org.

coordinated efforts among police, customs and environment agencies of all ten ASEAN member states. In 2004, the ASEAN ministers responsible for the implementation of CITES expressed the commitment of member states to improving implementation of the Convention.[41] At that time, Lao PDR was the only member state that had not acceded to the Convention, but the creation of ASEAN-WEN provided an impetus to ASEAN member states to strengthen legislative efforts and encouraged Lao PDR to accede to the Convention. Since the creation of ASEAN-WEN, Singapore has substantively amended its laws on wildlife trade. In 2006, Singapore passed the new Endangered Species (Import and Export) Act to impose harsher penalties on violators and provide officials with the right to inspect species in transit. In the same vein, Malaysia passed its International Trade in Endangered Species Act 2008 and its Wildlife Conservation Act 2010.

Wildlife crimes should and must be taken more seriously by law enforcement agencies in the region. The UN Office on Drugs and Crime in Asia recently listed wildlife crime as a core focus. With the recent establishment of the International Consortium on Combating Wildlife Crime, it offers hope that enforcement will be enhanced.[42]

[41] ASEAN Statement on CITES on the Occasion of the Thirteenth Meeting of Conference of Parties to CITES, Bangkok, October 11, 2004, at www.aseansec.org/16470.htm.

[42] The International Consortium on Combating Wildlife Crime www.cites.org/eng/prog/iccwc.php; see *ASEAN-WEN Regional Stakeholders Law & Policy Workshop on Wildlife Crime* December 8–10, 2014,

The drive for energy independence has led the Philippine government to push for the cultivation of jatropha, cassava, sugar cane, maize and sorghum for biofuel production, thus displacing traditional crop varieties. It is feared the expansion of biofuel crop production will encourage monocultures in the uplands, further depleting biodiversity. In reports prepared for the Food and Agriculture Organization, the Philippines[43] (and Thailand) noted loss of plant and animal genetic resources important to agriculture in the country. Genetic erosion of rice is a growing concern because the collection of indigenous rice species is quickly disappearing as rice paddies are urbanized and farmers exhibit increased preference for new prolific species. Extension of land for industrial and residential purposes has reduced the availability of traditional farming areas; indigenous cultivated plants and genetic resources for fruits are declining at a rapid rate. Increased imports of alien animals have resulted in increased ignorance of indigenous animal species. Local swamp buffalos are not only declining in numbers, but also crossbred with foreign species resulting in the loss and erosion of indigenous species.

The ACB was launched at the Ninth Informal ASEAN Ministerial Meeting on September 27, 2005. Its creation was

Faculty of Law, National University of Singapore, http://law.nus.edu.sg/apcel/workshops/ASEAN%20Legal%20Studies%20and%20Support%20Program%20to%20Fight%20Transnational%20Organized%20Wildlife%20Crime%20.pdf.

[43] The Philippines ratified the UNCBD and Cartagena Protocol, as well as the International Treaty on Plant Genetic Resources for Food and Agriculture (ITPGRFA) in 2006.

preceded by the ASEAN Regional Center for Biodiversity Conservation, which was funded by the European Commission and fostered collaborative efforts among member states, ASEAN and the European Commission (EC) partner institutions. In 2004, the EC approved a grant to support the establishment and operation of a new regional institution to strengthen capacity of ASEAN member states to devise and coordinate policies and strategies with national governments and regional and international organizations on matters related to biodiversity conservation and the sustainable use of natural resources.

Today, the ACB serves as the CBD's Clearing House Mechanism for the dissemination and integration of information on biodiversity in the region. In keeping with its mission to "champion biodiversity conservation in the region and enhance its global standing as a centre of excellence for biodiversity conservation,"[44] the ACB facilitates consolidation, access, analysis and promotion of regional biodiversity information, issues and initiatives of the ASEAN member states, and serves as a single portal for all information resources and applications. The ACB also houses databases for ASEAN Heritage Parks and protected areas and species in the region.

4.3.2 *Natural and cultural heritage*

ASEAN member states possess a very rich cultural background and history. Each state has enacted national

[44] ASEAN Centre for Biodiversity, *Mission*, www.aseanbiodiversity.org.

legislation[45] toward the protection of cultural sites, monuments and heritage. All ASEAN member states are now parties to the UNESCO Convention on the Protection of the World Cultural and Natural Heritage.

To date, Cambodia has two properties[46] inscribed on the World Heritage list, Indonesia has eight,[47] Lao PDR has two,[48] the Philippines has five,[49] Vietnam has seven[50] and Thailand has five.[51]

45 Antiquities and Treasure Trove Act 1967 (Brunei), Law on the Protection of Cultural Heritage 1996 (Cambodia), Indonesia Charter for Heritage Conservation 2003 (Indonesia), Law on National Heritage 2005 (Lao PDR), Antiquities Act 1976 and National Heritage Act 2005 (Malaysia), Protection and Preservation of Cultural Heritage Regions Law (Myanmar), National Cultural Heritage Act 2009 (Philippines), Preservation of Monuments Act (Singapore), Act on Ancient Monuments, Antiques, Objects of Art and Natural Museums 1961 (Thailand) and Law on Cultural Heritage 2001 (Vietnam).

46 Angkor and the Temple of Preah Vihear.

47 Komodo National Park, Lorentz National Park, Tropical Rainforest Heritage of Sumatra and Ujung Kulon National Park, Borobodur Temple Compounds, Prambanan Temple Compounds, Tropical Rainforest Heritage of Sumatra and Sangiran Early Man Site.

48 Town of Luang Prabang, and Vat Phou and Associated Ancient Settlements within the Champasak Cultural Landscape.

49 Tubbataha Reefs National Park, the Baroque Churches, the Rice Terraces of the Philippine Cordilleras, Puerto-Princesa Subterranean River National Park and the historic town of Vigan.

50 Central Sector of the Imperial Citadel of Thang Long – Hanoi, Citadel of the Ho Dynasty, Complex of Hue Monuments, Hoi, An Ancient Town, My Son Sanctuary and the natural sites of Ha Long Bay and Phong Nha-Ke Bang National Park.

51 Ban Chiang Archaeological Site, Dong Phayayen-Khao Yai Forest Complex, Historic City of Ayutthaya, Historic Town of Sukhothai and

On May 15, 2015, the Singapore Botanic Gardens was inscribed as a UNESCO World Heritage Site at the 39th session of the World Heritage Committee in Germany.[52]

In June 2012, Thailand made publicly known its displeasure at the UNESCO Committee's consideration of Cambodia's proposed management plan of the Preah Vihear Temple. Ownership of the temple was once hotly disputed between Thailand and Cambodia; in 1962, the International Court of Justice awarded the temple to Cambodia. Thailand announced its intention to withdraw from the World Heritage Convention at the 35th session of the UNESCO World Heritage Committee, in June 2011.[53]

With increasing urban development, there are concerns among NGOs of ASEAN countries that buildings and environments of historic interest and architectural merit are fast disappearing. On that note, the Jakarta Declaration on Architectural Heritage[54] concluded that: "Through the spirit of ASEAN Solidarity, a joint effort is deemed necessary to safeguard our Architectural

Associated Historic Towns and Thungyai-Huai Kha Khaeng Wildlife Sanctuaries.

52 www.sbg.org.sg/unesco/.

53 K. Alderman, "Thailand Denounces the 1972 UNESCO World Heritage Convention," *Cultural Property and Archaeology Law*, http://culturalpropertylaw.net/2011/06/30/thailand-denounces-the-1972-unesco-world-heritage-convention/. See also http://whc.unesco.org/en/news/772.

54 Jakarta Declaration on Architectural Heritage, Jakarta, March 15, 1991, www.unescobkk.org/fileadmin/user_upload/culture/cultureMain/Instruments/Jakarta_Declaration.pdf.

Heritage as a shared treasure of the communities in the Region." The Declaration endorsed the establishment of an ASEAN Federation on Architectural Heritage under ASEAN in the near future, and set out guidelines for education and training in the conservation of monuments, ensembles and sites.

4.4 Natural resources: Fresh and other sources of water and forests

4.4.1 Fresh water

The ASEAN region has abundant sources of water during some periods, while there are droughts at other times. With the exception of Singapore – once listed as a "water-scarce country" in 2006 but now self-sufficient in water because it has developed NEWater (which is not fresh water but recycled used water) and uses desalinated water – none of the ASEAN member states has had a shortage of water resources until recently when there have been droughts due to climate change. Hence, it can be said that there may be peiods of too much water and periods of drought. Such is the realtiy of today's climate.

The main issue in the region is the quality of the water supply because rivers in many cities are highly polluted due to industrial and sewerage discharges and garbage disposal. In particular, this section will trace the rise (and fall) of water management in Indonesia and Vietnam, examine the laudable efforts of Singapore and Cambodia and the challenges that face riparian states in the Lower Mekong Basin.

Cambodia

Decades of conflict had left a poor water supply system in Phnom Penh until the government enlisted an engineer, Ek Sonn Chan, to head the Phnom Penh Water Authority (PPWA) in 1993. Under Ek's leadership, PPWA developed strategies to improve water supply and water supply services, and imposed a tariff system based on volume consumed. In 1999, the Council of Ministers in Cambodia passed Sub-decree No. 27 on the Control of Water Pollution, which specified standards for effluent discharge; required licenses before discharges are allowed, and prohibited sewage, garbage and other pollutants to be discharged into public waters. Today, almost everyone in the capital receives potable water from taps twenty-four hours a day, with only 6 percent of water unaccounted for. All households and establishments are metered. Collections have increased from 50 to 100 percent. The PPWA and Ek have won many international awards for their laudable efforts. In 2006, the PPWA was tasked with bringing all of Cambodia's water supply to the same level as that in Phnom Penh. Ek remains in charge and is working hard to achieve what he had accomplished for Phnom Penh.[55]

Indonesia

In contrast, Indonesia's Clean Rivers Program, also known as Program Kali Bersih (PROKASIH), which received accolades

[55] www.rmaf.org.ph/Awardees/Biography/pdfbio/ChanEk.pdf.

in the 1990s,[56] has faltered with decentralization in Indonesia in 2001. A recent report states that nine of Indonesia's main rivers are contaminated with dangerously high levels of carbon dioxide due to improper disposal of industrial chemicals and agriculture and domestic waste. It is not for want of laws but a question of priorities and implementation in Indonesia. Indeed, the Water Resources Law[57] applies principles of integrated water resources management. Effective implementation of the law, however, requires integration with regulatory provisions on irrigation,[58] cooperation among local governments and between local and central government, a strengthening of institutional functionality at local and central government that includes water user associations, increasing capacity of local government in financing water resources management and the rehabilitation of river infrastructure and irrigation networks through public participation.[59]

In 2008, the Asian Development Bank, a Manila-based lender, agreed to provide "a $500m (£340m) loan package to the Indonesian government to support the restoration

[56] See R. Koestorer, "Proper Prokasih, the Indonesia River Care Programme" 1994, www.unescap.org/drpad/vc/conference/ex_id_14_ppi.htm; D. Wheeler and S. Afsar, *Going Public on Polluters in Indonesia: Bapedal's Proper Prokasih Program* 1996, http://siteresources.worldbank.org/nipr/work_paper/proper/index.htm.

[57] Law No. 7/2004.

[58] Government Regulation No. 20 of 2006 on Irrigation.

[59] See, for example, Indonesia's Water Resources Policy Reform Process No. 175, *Global Water Partnership ToolBox Integrated Water Resources Management* (2012), www.gwptoolbox.org/index.php?option=com_case&id=118.

of the Citarum River basin, which supports a population of 28 million people, delivers 20 [percent] of Indonesia's gross domestic product, and provides 80 [percent] of water supply to the capital, Jakarta."[60] The loan will allow "cultivation of an additional 61,700 acres (25,000 hectares) of rice paddy, benefiting 25,000 farming families," and also "aims to supply water to 200,000 more households in Jakarta."[61] Ultimately, the river management program funded by the Asian Development Bank will "increase Jakarta's water supply by 2.5 [percent] yearly, and benefit millions by resolving critical water shortages in Bandung, Indonesia's fourth largest city."[62]

Singapore

This country has gained global attention for good water governance and management. In just four decades, Singapore overcame water shortages despite polluted rivers and a lack of natural water resources. It cleaned up its rivers, imposed strict regulations on water pollution and invested in new technology for the clean-up and re-use of waste water as well as desalination plants. Singapore is one of the few countries in the world to harvest urban storm water for its

[60] J. Aldred, "Polluted Indonesia River to get $500m Clean-up," *The Guardian*, December 5, 2008, www.guardian.co.uk/environment/2008/dec/05/water-pollution. See also "Cleaning up Indonesia's Citarum Basin," ADB, October 2, 2012, www.adb.org/features/cleaning-indonesias-citarum-basin.

[61] Ibid.

[62] Ibid.

water supply, but it still continues to import water from its neighbor, the state of Johor, Malaysia, through two major water agreements. The first agreement (1961) provided for a fifty-year supply of water while the second agreement (1962) would provide a ninety-nine-year supply of water through to 2060. The first agreement expired in 2011. The government did not seek its renewal, instead emphasizing new measures for self-sufficiency.

The country has adopted an integrated water resources management approach and obtains its water from four sources: reservoirs and catchments, imported water, treated wastewater (NEWater)[63] and desalinated water.[64] All major estuaries are dammed to create reservoirs. By 2011, two-thirds of its land areas had become water catchments areas. In addition, the Public Utilities Board (PUB),[65] "aims to harness water from the remaining streams and rivulets near the shoreline using technology that can treat water of varying salinity"[66] to boost Singapore's water catchment area to 90 percent by 2060. Today, the country is 100 percent sewered. A license is required for trade effluent discharge, and emission limits are specified in the Environmental Protection

[63] NEWater is treated wastewater, primarily for non-potable industrial uses. See, for example, Singapore Government, "NEWater," www.pub.gov.sg/about/historyfuture/Pages/NEWater.aspx.

[64] Singapore's second desalination plant commenced operations in 2013. See www.pub.gov.sg/water/Pages/DesalinatedWater.aspx.

[65] See www.pub.gov.sg.

[66] Singapore Government, "The Singapore Water Story," www.pub.gov.sg/water/Pages/singaporewaterstory.aspx.

and Management Act, the Sewerage and Drainage Act, and their Trade Effluent Regulations.[67]

Vietnam

Water is central to the landscape, geography and history of Vietnam for it has always provided a food source to the people and security to the country. As the country progresses, however, environmentalists fear that inland freshwater ecosystems are taking a back seat to economic development projects. In addition, urbanization and the rapid formation of industrial zones have caused rivers and their surrounding basins to become polluted at an alarming level. Contamination also results from use of agricultural pesticides and fertilisers.[68] In 1998, the National Assembly passed the Law on Water Resources,[69] which stipulates management, protection, development and utilization of water resources, as well as control and mitigation of any adverse consequences caused by water.

While it is evident that Vietnam has instituted a regulatory structure to ensure sustainable use, protection and development of water resources, the current legal system

[67] See NEA Code of Practice on Pollution Control at http://app2.nea.gov.sg/codeofpractice.aspx.

[68] See, for example, H. Thang, *Water Pollution Management in Viet Nam River Basins: Challenges and Opportunities*, Viet Nam Environment Administration, http://asemwaternet.org/fileserver/forum/WPPOLLUT_07.pdf.

[69] The Law on Water Resources No. 08/1998/QH10, adopted in May 20, 1998.

for the protection of water resources is insufficient because laws, ordinances and secondary regulations are at odds with one another.[70] In June 2012, legislators debated the Law on Water Resources (as amended) during the third session of the 13th National Assembly.[71] Notably, these law makers recommended that harsher penalties should be imposed on violators of the law, and that the Government should "issue priority policies for handling demand for water in mountainous, remote, border and island areas, or areas with difficult socio-economic conditions that [do] not have access to clean water programs."[72]

Lower Mekong Basin

Cambodia, Lao PDR, Thailand and Vietnam share one of the largest and most productive inland fisheries in the world. All four states are members of the Mekong River Commission (MRC), established in 1995. In early 2011 the MRC endorsed two key strategies: the Integrated Water Resources Management (IWRM)-based Basin Development Strategy and the Mekong River Commission Strategic Plan 2011–2015.

70 Nguyen Thi Phuong Loan, "Legal Framework of the Water Sector in Vietnam," ZEF Working Paper Series 52 (2010), p. 83; and update in 2013 at www.academia.edu/5504082/The_Legal_Framework_of_Vietnam_s_Water_Sector_Update_2013.

71 "Law Makers Debate on Water Resources," *VietNam News*, June 1, 2012, http://en.baomoi.com/Home/sciencetechnology/vietnamnews.vnagency.com.vn/Law-makers-debate-on-water-resources/269879.epi; see also www.academia.edu/5504082/The_Legal_Framework_of_Vietnam_s_Water_Sector_Update_2013.

72 "Law Makers Debate on Water Resources," *VietNam News*.

The IWRM-based Basin Development Strategy presents opportunities for coordinated basin development and management and "provides the interconnection between national and basin planning."[73] The Strategy is a long-term (sixty-year) plan and postulates a number of different scenarios, including an analysis of climate change impacts, response to increasing risks of floods and droughts, and options for addressing the potential impacts of sea-level rise on the delta as part of long-term delta management. The Strategy relies on effective implementation of "basic processes of surface water and groundwater monitoring, water use permitting (of withdrawals and pollution discharges), compliance assurance of permit conditions and regulations, and maintaining a computerised water information system"[74] in all member countries. Only then can it provide a strong foundation for managing and developing water resources in the Lower Mekong Basin. Improving and sustaining these essential tasks will require additional financing, however. To enforce implementation of the Strategy, a Basin Action Plan was prepared in 2011. It comprises a regional action plan and four complementary and consistent national indicative plans, one for each member country of the MRC. Each plan includes a description of activities, methodologies, implementation and management responsibilities, milestones, deliverables, and costs and coordination requirements. The

[73] Mekong River Commission for Sustainable Development, *IWRM-based Basin Development Strategy for the Lower Mekong Basin*, November 29, 2010, p. 2, www.lowyinterpreter.org/file.axd?file=2010%2F12%2F101206+IWRM.pdf.

[74] Ibid., at p. 16.

preparation of the regional action plan will be led by the MRC and implemented through the MRC Strategic Plan for the period 2011 to 2015.

Under the guidance of experts on IWRM, the collaboration efforts by the four ASEAN member states in the Lower Mekong River is highly laudable, and should ensure that the waters of the Mekong and its rich ecosystems and food sources will continue to be sustainably managed. However, recent tensions have arisen between Lao PDR and Cambodia over the $3.5 billion Xayaburi Dam backed by Thailand, and to be built by Lao PDR. The Mekong River Commission had ruled that the dam project should not proceed until further assessments have been conducted, but Lao PDR appears to have disregarded the ruling.[75] While the proposed Lower Mekong Basin mainstream hydropower dams would benefit member countries in hydro-electricity sharing, there are uneven distributions of incremental impacts. Cambodia and Vietnam would be most affected by the risks, including reduced capture fisheries and changes in sediment transport. However, opportunities for irrigated agriculture, fisheries development, reduced flood damage, increased river-borne trade and tourism would be more evenly distributed among member countries. Managing the Mekong Basin, in line with IWRM principles, will require riparian countries to address cross-border issues through strong coordination and cooperation among countries. The Second Summit of the MRC

[75] *Bangkok Post*, "Laos denies lying about dam construction," July 22, 2012, www.bangkokpost.com/news/local/303668/laos-denies-lying-over-xayaburi-dam-construction.

(in March 2014) made no mention of the Xayaburi Dam,[76] while NGOs have set a one-year deadline to stop the dam.[77]

4.4.2 *Forests*

Only 5 percent of the world's forests are located in Southeast Asia, but the region accounts for nearly 25 percent of global forest loss over the last decade. Its forests are rich in biodiversity and are home to a large number of threatened and endangered species. Even more so than in other parts of the world, forests in the region are subject to a myriad of intensive, degrading pressures from: unsustainable forest management; clearing for conversion to monoculture plantations and mining activities; fires; small-scale agriculture encroachments; infrastructure development; wildlife poaching; illegal logging; and invasive alien species.[78] Individually, ASEAN member states have enacted laws to protect their forest resources and biological diversity, as well as to prohibit trade in endangered species. These laws also serve to establish protected areas, where biological diversity is given enhanced protection, and the emphasis is on protection of ecological systems. Each member state has its unique institutional and administrative structure: some states have a ministry that oversees the environment as a whole while

[76] See http://en.vietnamplus.vn/Home/Declaration-of-2nd-summit-of-Mekong-River-Commission/20144/48457.vnplus.

[77] See http://wwf.panda.org/wwf_news/?218410/NGOs-set-one-year-deadline-to-stop-Xayaburi-dam.

[78] The World Bank, *Environment in East Asia and Pacific: Forest Law Enforcement and Governance*, www.worldbank.org/eapfleg.

others divide the environment into sectors for which different bodies are responsible. In addition, the work of the ACB has been particularly important toward protected areas. In 2010, it provided gap analysis of terrestrial, coastal and marine protected areas in the region.

In Cambodia, ACB noted that there is "no overarching legislation for protected areas," and that most protected areas are "surviving with short-term planning only, represented by the annual operation plans."[79] Hence, Cambodia, with aid from the World Bank, has created new legislative frameworks to govern the management of land and forestry.[80] The Forest Concession Management and Control Pilot Project has aided Cambodia in establishing an effective logging concession management system, and reduced illegal logging. The Land Management and Administration Project has improved land security for citizens and created an efficient land market by providing a million families with land titles. Also, the Biodiversity and Protected Area Project helped build capacity to operate a well-managed national protected area system by providing the necessary framework for establishing local management systems for natural resources, and for resolving issues of land tenure, community user rights and resource utilization.

79 ASEAN Centre for Biodiversity, *Protected Areas Gap Analysis in the ASEAN Region*, 2010, www.aseanbiodiversity.org/index.php?option=com_flippingbook&view=book&id=22.

80 Forestry Administration, Laws, Decrees, Sub Decrees and Regulations Concerning Forestry, updated December 31, 2004, www.forestry.gov.kh/Law/Regulations_Eng.html.

In Indonesia, confusion and disputes over control and ownership of forests presents the greatest challenge in the management of forest estates, even though the country has a number of comprehensive laws on forestry.[81] Research on land use and remote sensing data revealed that significant areas of "Forest Zone" as defined by the Department of Forestry are in fact community planted agro-forests, agricultural lands or grasslands.[82] These areas are regulated as natural forests or lands to be reforested for timber production, thus many local communities who plant agro-forests on their customary land often find their access and rights to these lands heavily restricted by forest regulations. In a study[83] conducted by invitation of the World Bank, analysts recommend reclassifying land with no natural forest cover and recognizing community rights. Similarly, there has been an increased push toward recognizing community rights in forest management in the Philippines, Lao PDR, Thailand and Vietnam.

In the Philippines, the Department of the Environment and Natural Resources (DENR) has an extremely broad portfolio. It takes charge of a vast field of environmental

[81] Law No. 41/1999 is the main body of law regulating forests in Indonesia. The other laws include Government Regulation No. 6/2007 on Forest Governance and Formulation of Forest Management Plan, and Utilization of Forest; Government Regulation No. 76/2008 on Forest Reclamation; and Government Regulation No. 10/2010 on Procedure to Change the Usage and Function of Forest Area.

[82] A. Contreras-Hermosilla and C. Fay, *Strengthening Forest Management in Indonesia through Land Tenure Reform: Issues and Framework for Action*, 2005, www.forest-trends.org/documents/files/doc_107.pdf.

[83] Ibid.

management: pollution control and nature conservation of forests, lands, mineral resources, fisheries and other resources; air quality management; water management; solid waste management; environmental education; climate change adaptation and mitigation; and law enforcement. Similarly, the Ministry of Natural Resources and Environment in Malaysia is tasked with forest management, irrigation and drainage management, wildlife management, minerals management, environmental conservation and marine park management.

Singapore, however, divides the environment into two distinct sectors, pollution, and nature conservation, each managed by different bodies. The Ministry of Environment and Water Resources is in charge of pollution management and water resources while the National Parks Board under the Ministry of National Development is responsible for the management of parks, trees and nature reserves. Singapore's National Biodiversity Centre was established by the National Parks Board on May 22, 2006.[84] The National Biodiversity Centre serves as Singapore's one-stop center for biodiversity-related information and activities. Under the Ministry of National Development, the Urban Redevelopment Authority oversees land use planning while the Agri-Veterinary Authority administers wildlife laws, including regulation of trade in endangered species pursuant to CITES. The Agri-Veterinary Authority also regulates the fishing industry, as its primary role is to ensure the

[84] "About NBC" – see www.nparks.gov.sg/biodiversity/national-biodiversity-centre.

safety and security of food supplies. In 2010, Singapore proposed a Cities Biodiversity Index which was adopted at the Conference of the Parties on the Convention on Biodiversity in Nagoya.[85] The Singapore Index comprises three components: (i) biodiversity in the city; (ii) ecosystem services provided by native biodiversity in the city; and (iii) governance and management of biodiversity in the city. In this form, it would function as a monitoring tool.[86]

Whatever the structure may be, it is important from the context of effective management of the environment that administrative jurisdictions are clear and do not overlap. At the same time, there should be collaborative efforts among different institutions, and their officers should be provided with sufficient education and resources to effectively manage and implement laws and policies.

4.5 Marine and coastal resources

In 2010, the ASEAN Centre for Biodiversity conducted a gap analysis on protected areas in Southeast Asia by compiling assessments of terrestrial, coastal and marine protected areas of several participating ASEAN member states and various global datasets. According to their findings:

> Thailand registered the highest percentage of marine areas protected at 4.4 percent, followed by Philippines

[85] See www.cbd.int/authorities/gettinginvolved/cbi.shtml.

[86] See Draft User's Manual on the CDB website at www.cbd.int/doc/groups/cities/cities-draft-user-manual-singapore-index-2009-07-01-en.pdf.

> (2.5%), Malaysia (2%), and Indonesia (2%). Viet Nam (1.71%), Brunei Darussalam (1.4%) and Singapore (1.4%) had a little over one percent each of their respective marine protected areas while Myanmar has the smallest marine protected area coverage with only 0.31 percent. Consequently, out of the 82 Marine Key Biodiverse Areas (MKBA) identified in the region, 78 percent remain unprotected, indicating a significant representation gap. Ten percent are partially protected, signifying an ecological gap in the marine protected areas managed. Only 12 percent of the MKBAs are under protection but management concerns remain to be an issue.[87]

The Center's findings also revealed that while there has been a uniform increase in the amount of marine protected areas in the period from 1990 to 2000, there has also been a decline in the quality and quantity of coastal and marine habitats.[88]

As Southeast Asia is one of Earth's regions of the greatest biodiversity, many ASEAN member states have declared numerous marine parks and sanctuaries, and have passed laws to protect marine ecosystems and marine life such as sea turtles and dugongs. There are 153 marine conservation areas in Indonesia.[89] Malaysia has listed 128 marine protected areas and marine parks, and has passed laws to protect fisheries and marine mammals.[90] Myanmar has enacted laws to protect the threatened Irrawaddy Dolphin and the Burmese roof

[87] Protected Areas Gap Analysis in the ASEAN Region, 2010, at p. V, www.aseanbiodiversity.org/index.php?option=com_content&view=article&id=172&Itemid=179&current=110.

[88] Ibid., at p. VI.

[89] Ibid., at p. 18.

[90] Ibid., at p. 20.

terrapin while the Philippines has enacted a host of legislation to protect fisheries, aquatic animals and mammals in the country. Thailand has twenty-one declared marine national parks in the Gulf of Thailand and the Andaman Sea, with five more proposed.[91] Not all ASEAN member states have marine environment issues; the Lao PDR, a landlocked terrain, has no specific law on marine and coastal governance. Singapore has but one wetland reserve, no marine sanctuaries and no specific law to protect its marine life with the exception of corals (protected under the State Lands Act); it is unclear whether the Wild Animals and Birds Act applies to marine species.

4.6 Human settlements

Some of the world's mega-cities are sited in the ASEAN region; namely Jakarta, Bangkok, Ho Chi Minh City and Metro Manila. As populations continue to rise, the impact on resources will be enormous. There is a need to ensure that cities are sustainable. While new cities (so-called eco-cities) can be built in accordance with ecologically sound and sustainable methods, major challenges continue to confront existing cities, which are crowded and highly polluted.

A key challenge for all cities is to provide their citizens with a safe and reliable supply of food, water and essential services. There is a need for good roads and efficient public transportation systems, modern sanitation, effective waste management (municipal solid waste disposal, hazardous

[91] Ibid., at p. 22.

wastes treatment facilities, etc.), decent and affordable housing, good communication facilities (to reduce the need to travel), protection of natural and cultural heritage and sustainable use of natural resources, to ensure a good quality of life.

These challenges facing crowded cities are now exacerbated by climate change, which brings about harsher and more inclement weather. Hence, all member states should re-examine their vulnerability to increased frequency and intensity of storms and floods, and it will require sound and comprehensive land use planning and a review of vulnerable areas. While the solutions will differ depending on the resources and needs of each city, cities do need an environmental management system (EMS) much like that in the standards established by ISO 14000. Indeed, some have obtained ISO 14001 certification.[92]

As urban populations continue to expand, conflicts between conservation and development will escalate. An Environmental Impact Assessment (EIA) is a useful tool to ensure preservation of environmentally sensitive areas, protection of biological diversity and heritage sites. However, the EIA has to be well crafted and complemented by access to information, access to justice and public participation. Indonesia, Malaysia, the Philippines, Thailand and Vietnam

[92] In 2003, the International Environmental Technology Centre developed its "Environmental Management Systems and ISO 14001 for Cities" using Tokyo as illustration, and produced a Toolkit. Since then, many Japanese cities have obtained certification, as well as Dallas, Seattle and Charlottesville in the USA, and Toronto and Edmonton in Canada.

have EIA laws but implementation in these member states has been less than satisfactory. In Indonesia, national legislation details procedures for appraisals and entails a top-down approach that involves sectoral ministers and provincial governments. However, as in many developing countries, actual implementation remains an issue because such EIA procedures are "viewed as obstructive to development."[93] The EIA system in the Philippines has also been severely criticized.[94] In Vietnam, implementation of EIA laws is hindered by "lack of capacity in provinces and ministries and significant weaknesses in applying environment provisions subsequent to approval of EIA studies."[95]

Cambodia has recently drafted legislation on EIA.[96] Brunei has indicated that an EIA law will soon be passed for large-scale housing projects.[97] Singapore has yet to pass

93 Environmental Impact Analysis under the Indonesian Law Concerning Environmental Management at www.unescap.org/drpad/vc/orientation/legal/2D_std_ido.htm.

94 See, for example, M. Villaluz, "Advancing the EIA system in the Philippines," *UNEP EIA Training Resource Manual: Case Studies from Developing Countries*, www.unep.ch/etu/publications/35)%20257%20to%20260.pdf.

95 The World Bank, "Environment in East Asia and Pacific: Environmental Impact Assessments (EIA) and Safeguard Policies," www.worldbank.org/eap.

96 According to a copy of the EIA draft law, fines of 100 million riel, or about $25,000, and prison terms of three years will be imposed on individuals and firms that fail to submit an EIA on any development project. See "Law Drafted to Enforce Environmental Reports," Open Development Cambodia, January 13, 2013, www.opendevelopmentcambodia.net/tag/draft-eia-law/.

97 "New Law on Environmental Impacts of Large Scale Housing Projects Soon," *The Brunei Times*, March 11, 2012,

specific legislation on EIA. Although EIAs are conducted on an ad hoc basis when deemed warranted by the government, there is no right to view them. Like Singapore, Lao PDR lacks EIA law and EIAs are conducted on an ad hoc basis without proper guidelines, transparency or public participation.

4.7 Atmosphere

In the cities of ASEAN, it has been found that air pollution from mobile sources accounts for as much as 70 percent of ambient emissions, with industrial emissions accounting for the remaining 30 percent. Air pollution also results from the practice of seasonal burning by farmers and indigenous communities, as well as the clearing of forests for oil palm plantations and the pulp and paper industry – these activities all contribute to the haze in the region.

Clean Air Asia was established in 2001 as the premier air quality network for Asia by the Asian Development Bank, World Bank and the U.S. Agency for International Development (USAID). Its mission is to promote better air quality and livable cities by translating knowledge to policies and actions that reduce air pollution and greenhouse gas emissions from transport, energy and other sectors.[98] Headquartered in Manila, it has country networks in Indonesia and Vietnam. In 2006, its Clean Air Initiative for Asian Cities (CAI-Asia) Center led a comprehensive study on

www.bt.com.bn/business-national/2012/03/11/new-law-environmental-impact-large-scale-housing-projects-soon.

[98] http://cleanairasia.org/portal/aboutus.

urban air quality management through various country synthesis reports. It found that air pollution levels were highest in Thailand and Vietnam. The study found that each ASEAN member state experiences pollution from ambient and stationary sources, but not all member states have enacted laws to manage pollution from such sources. Indonesia, Malaysia, Thailand, Philippines and Singapore had such laws. Clean Air Asia then embarked on studies of air pollution management in both large and smaller cities in various Asian states, including ASEAN member states, evaluating air pollution levels and recommending management plans involving the government and the private sector.

In Indonesia, the Ministry of Environment conducted Urban Air Quality Evaluations in 2007, 2008 and 2011 as part of the Blue Sky Program to implement Environmentally Sustainable Transportation.[99] This focused only on urban transportation, recommending local legislation on air quality management and the development of environmentally sustainable transportation through the Indonesian municipalities network.[100] In the Philippines, the Partnership for Clean Air initiative also focused on pollution from motor vehicles, and for 2012–14, it promoted Electric Vehicles and Non-Motorized Forms of Mobility, Tricycle Upgrading and Anti-Smoke Belching Campaigns.[101]

99 http://cleanairasia.org/portal/countrynetworks/indonesia.

100 http://cleanairasia.org/portal/sites/default/files/Urban_AQ_Evaluation_in_Indonesia_2011_Blue_Sky_Program_Vol1.pdf.

101 http://cleanairasia.org/portal/countrynetworks/philippines.

In 2009, CAI-Asia started a German-assisted project for clean air in smaller ASEAN cities (population 50,001 to 1.5 million). The report on Thailand (2009) focused on both ambient air pollution and industrial air pollution.[102] PM10 was found to be a major pollutant, as well as sulphur dioxide from industries and power plants. Thailand's laws were found to be less stringent than the World Health Organization guidelines but prosecutions have been brought against factories that have caused severe air pollution.[103] Thailand has established a national ambient air quality monitoring network comprising some sixty-three continuous air monitoring stations in twenty-three provinces, focusing on the big cities and major industrial sites. It has phased out lead in gasoline, as well as the two-stroke motorcycle and seeks to monitor vehicle emissions and improve fuel quality standards. Its management plan for air quality seeks to impose ambient air quality standards, emissions standards, diesel emissions reductions, and to manage high polluting buses and trucks with an inspection and maintenance program. It also seeks to control and reduce burning in communities, agricultural areas and forests and to implement the ASEAN Haze Agreement. A draft Fire and Haze Master Plan (2012–2016) was agreed in principal by the National Committee on Fire and Haze Control (chaired by the Minister of Natural

[102] www.citiesforcleanair.org/documents/THAILAND_GTZ_COUNTRY_PROFILE_FINAL.pdf.

[103] *Kum Inkumpa* v. *Electricity Generating Authority*, Administrative Court Judgment No. 60 -77/2552 (2009) and No. 64/2548 (2003) – *Mae Moh* case, Lamphun District.

Resources and Environment) to be put to the Cabinet for approval. It includes measures targeted at the agricultural community to encourage them to refrain from burning and to promote best practices. Bangkok has developed a comprehensive action plan on Global Warming Mitigation, which aims to bring down greenhouse gas levels by 15 percent. For the smaller cities in Thailand, ten Pollution Control Areas have been declared.

In Vietnam, the CAI-Asia Center worked with the government to formulate a roadmap on cleaner fuels and vehicles, together with UNEP's Partnership Programme for Clean Fuels and Vehicles. Under the roadmap, automobiles will be required to comply with Euro 4 emission standards by January 1, 2017, with further tightening to Euro 5 emission standards starting January 1, 2022. Motorcycles manufactured, assembled or newly imported will be required to comply with Euro 3 emission standards beginning January 1, 2017. Parallel to these efforts, the government is also set to improve fuel quality standards by leapfrogging to Euro 4 beginning January 1, 2016, and eventually moving up to Euro 5 by January 1, 2021.[104]

A 2006 report by CAI-Asia on Cambodia found rapid deterioration in air quality in Cambodia's growing urban centers. It highly recommended the need for investment to build capacity in managing this challenge, such as regulations for cleaner fuels, emission standards for new vehicles, monitoring equipment and controls on large stationary sources. These actions require a suitable legal

[104] http://cleanairasia.org/portal/node/7530.

framework, with clean air quality goals as a priority.[105] In the case of Lao PDR, CAI-Asia (2006) identified that there was no specific legal framework for air quality management. When air quality sampling was conducted, 4 to 13 percent of the measurements failed to comply with the 2005 World Health Organization 24-hour guideline standards. Sources of particulate-matter emissions include diesel-powered vehicles, open fires, cooking, garbage burning and slash-and-burn cultivation in the surrounding areas, plus re-suspended road dust. CAI-Asia thus worked on the roadmap, "Towards a Clean Air Plan for Vientiane", published in May 2010.[106]

By December 2012, Clean Air Asia's Report *10 Years of Partnership* reported that Brunei, Cambodia and Lao PDR had established national air quality standards.[107]

CAI-Asia's most recent report for ASEAN is on Myanmar (2014).[108] As in the case of Cambodia, it called for the establishing of air quality goals including national ambient air quality standards and clean fuels. It called for cities to lead the development of air quality management policies in their area of jurisdiction, and for the Yangon City Development Committee (YCDC) to take the lead, as it has the mandate for planning, development and general management and is

105 cleanairasia.org/portal/system/files/documents/cambodia_0.pdf.

106 www.citiesforcleanair.org/documents/FinalRoadMapVientianeMay17_2010.pdf.

107 Clean Air Asia, *Ten Years of Partnership*, December 2012, http://cleanairasia.org/portal/sites/default/files/documents/Clean_Air_Asia_Annual_Report_-_FINAL.pdf.

108 http://cleanairasia.org/portal/sites/default/files/myanmar_camp_-_final_report_-_june_2014_final_1.pdf.

the authorized body for urban environmental management of Yangon city.

The challenge for ASEAN cities is to ensure that urban development and industrialization are carefully planned. The regulation of vehicular emissions alone is inadequate. Emissions from stationary sources must also be regulated. Pollutive factories must be sited away from residential and commercial areas; vehicular emissions must be reduced by mandating the use of cleaner fuel, newer vehicles and improvements in the public transport sector. Laws need to be passed setting out emission standards and planning controls, and the infrastructure including air monitoring systems must be put in place.[109] The burning of agricultural and municipal waste must be carefully controlled, and alternatives considered. The ASEAN Agreement on Transboundary Pollution needs to be implemented at the national level and slash-and-burn cultivation as well as the burning of garbage must be carefully managed.

Singapore has comprehensive planning laws on the siting of its industries, and has implemented strict policies to control the number of motor vehicles on its roads, with the imposition of high import taxes, road pricing and other innovative mechanisms.[110] Singapore, Malaysia and the Philippines are encouraging the use of clean fuels and hybrid and electric cars.

[109] The most sophisticated air monitoring systems were found in Indonesia, Malaysia, Philippines, Singapore and Thailand.

[110] See Lye, "Environmental Taxation in the Management of Traffic in Singapore." See also www.lta.gov.sg/content/ltaweb/en/roads-and-motoring/owning-a-vehicle.html.

In the Philippines, biofuels are especially touted as sources of clean fuel.[111]

Improvements in the transport infrastructure for urban areas are needed, particularly the building of mass rapid transit systems for cities. This will reduce the number of vehicles on the road and thus reduce air pollution, as well as resolve the problem of massive traffic jams in cities. Singapore has an efficient and well-planned mass rapid transport (MRT) system. Jakarta started to build its mass rapid rail transport system in 2012.[112] There are plans to improve Manila's Metro Rail Transit system, to double its current capacity by acquiring additional light rail vehicles. Malaysia has an MRT system in its capital city, Kuala Lumpur, and plans a further three-line MRT system located in Klang Valley, Kuala Lumpur. The MRT will be integrated with the LRT, Monorail, KTM Komuter and intra/intercity buses.[113]

111 The Philippines Biofuels Act of 2006 (RA 9367) mandated the blending of biodiesel and ethanol in all locally distributed diesel and gasoline (currently at 2 percent and 10 percent, respectively). Sugar cane and coconut oil are the preferred Philippine ethanol and biodiesel feedstocks, respectively. See http://gain.fas.usda.gov/Recent%20GAIN%20Publications/Biofuels%20Annual_Manila_Philippines_10-22-2014.pdf.

112 www.railway-technology.com/projects/jakarta-rapid-rail/. A government study found that "roads in Jakarta grow at a rate less than 1% a year while more than 1,000 new automobiles a day are launched on the city streets."

113 The project was announced in December 2010 by the Government of Malaysia, and was launched on 8 July 2011. See www.spad.gov.my/projects/klang-valley-mass-rapid-transit; and hwww.railwaystrategies.co.uk/article-page.php?contentid=18296&issueid=508.

The efforts by the Clean Air Initiative mentioned above are laudable. Properly implemented, they will help ensure the sustainable development of the newer ASEAN member states even as they seek to industrialize and urbanize.[114]

4.8 Appraisal of integration through law

Since the emergence of multilateral environmental agreements and the recommendations of Agenda 21, the ASEAN member states have individually enacted a substantial body of environmental legislation. While the laws constitute a congruent body of norms, it cannot yet be said that they are aligned to work in tandem to advance the policies and programs of ASEAN. This is largely because the laws are being assigned to different ministries in each state, and there are few environmental law experts skilled or experienced in applying and integrating application of the laws. Environmental law, because it is already enacted and being applied (albeit insufficiently) can provide a foundation for the integration of states within ASEAN. This is seen most clearly in the realm of protected natural and cultural heritage, or wildlife enforcement laws. ASEAN needs to harmonize the designation of focal points, or responsible national agencies and officials in each country so that the same "team" of government officers can cooperate across the entire ASEAN region. Where

114 At its most recent meeting in Singapore, members discussed the necessity of harmonized quality standards for fuels and vehicles in ASEAN. See http://cleanairasia.org/portal/node/12690 (2015).

capacity to implement common environmental obligations is lacking, ASEAN needs to prioritize education and training and resource allocation. The environmental laws of ASEAN member states are evidence that there is a sound platform for regional integration through law, but while the legislation is necessary, it is not sufficient to advance such integration very quickly. In the case of the environmental pillar of sustainable development, the test of integration through law will be when the environmental degradation trends are abated and patterns of sustainable development become clear. Greater national efforts toward attaining sustainability will be required.

Chapter 5

ASEAN collaboration towards environmental sustainability

> ASEAN shall promote sustainable development so as to ensure the protection of the region's environment, the sustainability of its natural resources, and the preservation of its cultural heritage and the high quality of life of its people.
>
> ASEAN Charter, Article 1(9)[1]

ASEAN's agenda for developing environmental policy and law began in 1978 (ASEAN Sub-Regional Environment Programme, Phase I) not long after the Stockholm Conference on the Human Environment ushered in the modern era of international environmental law in 1972.[2] The journey from 1978 culminating in the Cha-Am Hua Hin Declaration on the ASEAN Roadmap for an ASEAN Community 2009–2015 established the interlocking ASEAN Political-Security Community (APSC), ASEAN Economic Community (AEC) and ASEAN Socio-Cultural Community (ASCC), and the Initiative for ASEAN Integration Strategic Framework and IAI Work Plan 2 (2009–2015) intended to bring Cambodia, Lao PDR, Myanmar and Vietnam to a level

[1] ASEAN Charter, Article 1(9).

[2] UNEP Declaration of the United Nations Conference on the Human Environment, Stockholm, June 16, 1972, www.unep.org/Documents.Multilingual/Default.asp?documentid=97&articleid=1503.

where they are able to implement the Roadmap. The ASCC Council oversees the overall implementation of the ASCC and ensures coordination and cooperation across all other communities.

It is not possible to survey all the areas of work envisaged in the ASCC and other Communities on environmental sustainability. This chapter traces the cooperation and collaboration within ASEAN itself, as well as with organizations outside ASEAN. These measures complemented and helped to reinforce or even to stimulate the establishment of national environmental law and programs in the various ASEAN member states, described above in Chapter 4. In assessing the various levels of environmental integration, this chapter evaluates the gaps and obstacles along ASEAN's path toward building an integrated environmental sustainability system. A significant approach that underpins all decisions is the ASEAN Way, which has its origin in the Treaty of Amity and Cooperation in Southeast Asia of 1976.[3] The Treaty provides a set of norms for promoting cooperation in furtherance of peace, harmony and stability.

Regional security has become more complex than appeared to be the case in 1976. Concerns for traditional military security, as evidenced in the Indochinese and Vietnam Wars, is matched by non-traditional concerns. Beyond issues of organized crime, piracy, drug trafficking or terrorism, ASEAN

[3] K.-L. Koh, *ASEAN Environmental Law, Policy and Governance*, vol. I. (World Scientific, 2009), p. 713; K.-L. Koh and S. Karim, "The Role of ASEAN in Shaping Regional Environmental Protection," in P. Hirsch (ed.), *Routledge Handbook of the Environment in South East Asia* (Routledge, in press).

member states have been confronted by increasing numbers of new and emerging transnational environmental crises, including transboundary air and water pollution, toxic chemical waste dumping and trade, pandemic environmental public health threats (e.g. SARS, Avian Flu and H1N1), syndicated illegal wildlife trade in endangered species and climate change impacts. Some of these emerging issues have now become "new norms." One of the most significant developments in ASEAN environmental law in the last decade is "securitization" of transboundary challenges (including environmental threats), now known regionally as "non-traditional security" (NTS) issues under the APSC Blueprint.

The ASEAN approach regarding NTS issues constitutes a timely response in accordance with the principles of comprehensive security under Pillar I. The rationale of comprehensive security is that it "goes beyond the requirements of traditional security" and takes into account non-traditional aspects vital to regional and national resilience, such as environmental dimensions of development. Such issues often arise at short notice and, in the case of pandemics, with a high rate of transmission across borders. While prevention is difficult, coping mechanisms can be developed. Because unilateral national solutions are often inadequate, these issues require regional and multilateral cooperation, as has been documented by scholarly research conducted by political scientists and experts in international relations.[4] However,

[4] See S. Rajaratnam School of International Studies (RSIS) Centre for Non-Traditional Security (NTS) Studies, *RSIS Centre for Non-Traditional Security Studies Year in Review 2012* at www.rsis.edu.sg/publications/rsis-publications/rsis-publications-annual-reviews/.

there is a dearth of research in the context of environmental law. Some pioneering work on the legal perspective has been pursued in the ASEAN context.[5]

By framing NTS issues under Pillar I, instead of under Pillar III where most environmental issues are subsumed, ASEAN could elevate and prioritize these issues as requiring enhanced cooperation among all stakeholders and mobilize financial resources. An example under Pillar I is that of ASEAN's agreement to enhance effective and early response at the political and operational levels when activating disaster management arrangements to assist affected countries in the event of major disasters, and to enhance

5 K.-L. Koh, "The Discourse of Environmental Security in the ASEAN Context," in B. Jessup and K. Ruberstein (eds.), *Environmental Discourses in Public and International Law* (Cambridge University Press, 2012) at pp. 218–37; K.-L. Koh, "Transboundary and Global Environmental Issues: The Role of ASEAN in Transnational Environmental Law," *Transnational Environmental Law* 1(1) (March 13, 2012), pp. 1–16; K.-L. Koh and Md. S. Karim, "South East Asian Environmental Legal Governance," in S. Alam, J. Hossain Bhuiyan, T. Chowdhury, E. Techera (eds.), *Routledge Handbook of International Environmental Law* (Routledge Taylor & Francis Group, 2012) at pp. 461–77; K.-L. Koh and N. A. Robinson, "Strengthening Sustainable Development and Institutional Frameworks: Lessons from the 'ASEAN Way,'" *Singapore Journal of International & Comparative Law* 6 (2002), pp. 640–82; K.-L. Koh and Nicholas A. Robinson, "Regional Environment Governance: Examining the Association of Southeast Asian Nations (ASEAN) Model," in Daniel C. Esty and Maria H. Ivanova (eds.), *Global Environmental Governance* (Yale University Press, 2002); K.-L. Koh, "Towards an Effective ASEAN Environmental Governance for Sustainable Development?" *Asian Review of Public Administration*, 20 (1–2) (2008), pp. 35–59.

civilian-military coordination in order to provide effective and timely response to major natural disasters.[6] Because the approach to NTS issues commands enhanced cooperation, member states find it increasingly difficult to take an "isolationist stance." The earlier ASEAN concerns for sovereignty gave way to calls for urgent measures of regional cooperation. The impacts of climate change will elevate concern for NTS environmental issues, and the ASEAN Way will probably adapt to the demands of changing regional trends.

In 2012, The United Nations "Rio+20" Conference on Sustainable Development advanced the notion that an integrated national, regional and international approach is necessary to tackle transboundary and/or transnational problems.[7] Such an approach is already central to ASEAN's role in dealing with issues under Pillar I of the APSC Blueprint. Indeed, ASEAN has collaborated with Australia, the European Union, United States, China, Japan, Republic of South Korea and other members of the international community and has developed several environmental instruments to address transnational/transboundary environmental issues that have surfaced in the region. However, ASEAN does not (yet) operate from a central commission or regional parliament, nor does it prosecute through a regional court or other judicial tribunal, as the European Union does. ASEAN primarily

[6] ASEAN Political-Security Community Blueprint 2009, www.asean.org/archive/5187-18.pdf.

[7] Agenda Item 10, Rio+20 United Nations Conference on Sustainable Development (Rio de Janeiro) UN Doc A/CONF.216/L.1 (2012).

still relies on the will of individual member states to ensure the success of implementation of any ASEAN instruments, including those that may be developed for NTS issues. Until 2007, ASEAN lacked status as a legal person in international law. The ASEAN members are progressively strengthening ASEAN, and when their political will is aligned, ASEAN can be very effective, as illustrated by ASEAN's policy decisions for sustainability (see text box, ASEAN policy decisions for sustainability below).

5.1 Cooperation before the ASEAN Charter of 2007

At ASEAN's roots are the regional concern for both political security and economic pursuits. As noted above, the environment was not a consideration when ASEAN was established in 1967. Nonetheless, the ASEAN member states had begun to enact their initial environmental laws in the 1970s, and sensitivity to the issues was growing. ASEAN's earliest initiative in environmental cooperation began in 1976 when the United Nations Economic and Social Commission for Asia and the Pacific sent a team to the five founding ASEAN member states to determine the type of environmental issues that had so far arisen. Based on the data collected, the ASEAN Experts Group on the Environment drafted the ASEAN Sub-Regional Environment Programme (ASEP) I, with assistance from the United Nations Environment Programme (UNEP) in 1978. Over some thirty-one years, the ASEP were updated a number of times to accommodate new issues and priority areas. Among the priority areas identified and proposed as national activities in ASEP I, II and III (1978–92) were: environmental management including environmental impact assessment; nature conservation and terrestrial ecosystems; marine environment; industry and environment; environmental education and training; and environmental information.

In an effort to respond to the specific recommendations of Agenda 21 calling for priority actions in the region, ASEAN formulated the ASEAN Strategic Plan of Action on the Environment.[8] This Plan comprised ten strategies to:

> introduce policy measures and promote institutional development that will encourage integration of environmental factors in all developmental processes both at the national and regional levels; to establish long-term goals on environmental quality and work towards harmonized environmental quality standards for the ASEAN region; to harmonize policy directions and enhance operational and technical cooperation on environmental matters, and undertake joint actions to address common environmental problems.[9]

[8] Strategic Plan of Action on the Environment 1994–1998, http://environment.asean.org/index.php?page=overview:poa:spae.

[9] Ibid.

The strategies proposed included the establishment of a regional framework on biological diversity conservation and the sustainable utilization of its components.[10]

In the years that followed, ASEAN leaders adopted the ASEAN Hanoi Plan of Action[11] for the period 1999 to 2004, and the ASEAN Vientiane Action Programme[12] for the period 2004 to 2010. Both action plans addressed priority areas for the environment in the region, and can be considered as a continuum from ASEPs through to 2010, with refinements at different stages. In particular, the focus was on a number of factors aimed at bringing about ASEAN's progress on regional cooperation and integration by strengthening coordination among member countries, setting deadlines for urgent issues such as the Indonesia Haze and identifying crucial environmental issues.[13] The Vientiane Action Programme has since been replaced by the ASCC Blueprint[14], which came into effect in 2009.

[10] See K.-L. Koh, "ASEAN Environmental Protection in Natural Resources Sustainable Development Divergences and Convergence," in Asian Law Institute, *3rd ASLI Conference 2006: The Development of Law in Asia: Convergence versus Divergence*, Shanghai, Peoples Republic of China May 25–26, 2006.

[11] Hanoi Plan of Action, Kuala Lumpur, December 15, 1997, www.asean.org/asean/asean-summit/item/hanoi-plan-of-action. See Koh, *ASEAN Environmental Law, Policy and Governance*, vol. I, pp. 409–74.

[12] Vientiane Action Programme 2004–2010, Vientiane, November 29, 2004, www.aseansec.org/VAP-10th%20ASEAN%20Summit.pdf.

[13] C. Habito, F. Aldaba and O. Templo, *An Assessment Study on the Progress of ASEAN Regional Integration: The Ha Noi Plan of Action Toward ASEAN Vision 2020*, Ateneo Center for Economic Research and Development 2004, www.asean.org/aadcp/repsf/docs/03-006b-ExecutiveSummary.pdf.

[14] ASEAN Socio-Cultural Community Blueprint, Jakarta, 2009, www.asean.org/archive/5187-19.pdf.

ASEAN policy decisions for sustainability[15]

ASEAN's policy imperatives are set out at various times in soft law instruments. Among the main soft law instruments that assist member states in formulating their environmental policies and also in integrating environmental laws within the region are:

- Manila Declaration on the ASEAN Environment, 1981,[16] which ensures, as far as practicable, that environmental considerations are taken into account in development efforts, both ongoing and future. The Declaration encourages the enactment and enforcement of environmental protection measures in the ASEAN countries.
- Jakarta Resolution on Sustainable Development, 1987,[17] which integrates environmental considerations into the broader context of social and economic development. With the Brundtland Commission's report in 1978, *Our Common Future*,[18] the term "sustainable development" was brought to the fore of public consciousness. ASEAN took note of the call for greater concern for environmental dimensions of development.

15 Excerpt previously published in N. A. Robinson, "Strengthening Sustainable Development in Regional Inter-Governmental Governance: Lessons from the 'ASEAN Way'," *Pace Law Faculty Publication*, Paper 371 (2002).

16 Manila Declaration on the ASEAN Environment, Manila, April 30, 1981, www.aseansec.org/6077.htm.

17 Jakarta Resolution on Sustainable Development, Jakarta, October 30, 1987, www.aseansec.org/6081.htm.

18 UN World Commission on Environment and Development, *Our Common Future* (Oxford University Press, 1987).

The commitment of ASEAN to promoting regional cooperation to achieve sustainable development was reiterated in the Preamble to the Jakarta Resolution. It recognized both that the development processes in ASEAN must be accelerated to meet growing need and to provide a good quality of life, and that these processes could only be sustained if the natural resources were not degraded. It stressed the utilization of natural resources to meet the needs of present and future generations, and called for an *integrated approach*. The Preamble underlined that ASEAN members were intensely aware that international and regional cooperation must be heightened and that it was the duty of states to develop sustainable development in terms of the Stockholm Declaration and other environmental law instruments.

Other policy guidelines laid down by ASEAN have been used in the formulation of the various ASEAN programs and plans of action. Thus, for example, before formulating the ASEAN Strategic Plan of Action on the Environment, the ASEAN senior officials on the environment at its fourth meeting in Bangkok, in July 1993, reviewed past policies, some of which were still legitimate. The policy guidelines contained in a number of ASEAN soft law instruments had in fact been reflected in Phase I of ASEP way back in 1978.[19] These and other ASEAN instruments on policy imperatives for a sustainability transition in environment

[19] These were in the Manila Declaration on the ASEAN Environment 1981, Bangkok Declaration on the ASEAN Environment, 1984: Jakarta Resolution on Sustainable Development, 1987; and Kuala Lumpur Accord on Environment and Development, 1990.

and development focused on incorporating environmental factors into economic evaluations. The sum total of these various policies may be summarized thus:

- There should be an integrated approach to implement an ASEAN development strategy, to harmonize environmental quality standards as well as transboundary pollution prevention and abatement practices.
- Policy guidelines are to be adopted for the following areas:

  (i) Environment management – e.g. use of environmental impact assessments (EIAs) and of optimal land use plans, town and country planning or zoning plans.
  (ii) Nature conservation – e.g. develop new practicable approaches for preserving forests, wildlife and ecological systems; monitor the quality of the environment and natural resources to enable compilation of ASEAN state of the environment reports.
  (iii) Marine conservation – e.g. develop practicable methods for managing pollution discharges.
  (iv) Industry – e.g. ensure reasonable control of waste discharges from the earliest stages of project formulation; encourage recycling of waste; develop suitable systems for control of toxic and hazardous waste.
  (v) Education and training – e.g. enhance public awareness; introduce environmental subjects in schools and universities; provide technical training in environmental information systems; develop

comprehensive environmental systems to facilitate decision-making; establish monitoring programs for surveillance of sensitive environmental resources; promote use of remote sensing to establish a database with respect to wider involvement in environmental management – promote cooperation between governments, NGOs, universities and business communities within ASEAN.

(vi) Environmental legislation – e.g. develop appropriate legislation to support the proper management and development of the environment.

(vii) Enhanced ASEAN joint action – e.g. closer cooperation of the then ASEAN countries to act in unison in incorporating environmental factors in economic evaluations to provide a better foundation for natural resource management.

(viii) International cooperation – e.g. establish cooperation with developed and other developing countries and international agencies for transfer of technology and share experiences in the management of the environment.

5.2 The ASEAN Charter and beyond

The ASEAN Charter provides ASEAN with the advantages of a much-needed legal personality.[20] The Charter

[20] R. Severino (ed.), *Framing the ASEAN Charter: An ISEAS Perspective* (ISEAS Publication, 2005).

defines institutions and mechanisms for strengthening compliance in all areas including the environment, and helps to enhance development of ASEAN environmental law.[21] With reference to environmental law, the Preamble of the Charter resolves to "ensure sustainable development for the benefit of present and future generations and to place the well-being, livelihood and welfare of the peoples at the centre of the ASEAN community building process."[22] Environmental protection, as a pillar of sustainable development, has moved to the core of ASEAN's purpose and legal being. Despite this, environmental integration remains a secondary theme, an element of NTS or human rights (e.g. right to water) or as natural heritage in socio-cultural contexts. It remains for ASEAN's implementing framework to embrace the environment as a top theme in its own right, as the UN 2002 Johannesburg Plan of Implementation provides.

Since its inception, the Charter has supported a radical restructuring of ASEAN's organizational framework, fulfilling the ASEAN Vision 2020 of "One Vision, One Identity and One Caring and Sharing Society." This is of great significance because it led to the creation of new entities such as the ASEAN Coordinating Council and ASEAN Human Rights Body. These structures are aligned with the three Pillars (namely, the APSC, AEC and ASCC) and allow for effective

[21] Ibid.

[22] Charter of the Association of Southeast Asian Nations, Singapore, November 20, 2007, www.aseansec.org/21069.pdf.

cooperation and coordination of environmental law, policy and governance in ASEAN.

5.3 Implementing the Roadmap for an ASEAN Community 2009–2015

At the 14th ASEAN Summit in Cha-am, Thailand, ASEAN leaders agreed to adopt the APSC Blueprint, the AEC Blueprint, the ASCC Blueprint and the Initiative for ASEAN Integration Work Plan II (2009–2015) as the Roadmap for an ASEAN Community from 2009 to 2015.[23] The Roadmap served to inaugurate an ASEAN community across each of ASEAN's three mutually reinforcing pillars: (a) political-security relations, (b) economic relations and (c) socio-cultural relations. Each ASEAN member state was to ensure timely implementation of each instrument.[24]

In keeping with ASEAN's goal to ensure environmental sustainability in the region, the ASCC Blueprint[25] outlines environmental strategies to, inter alia, address global environmental issues, manage and prevent transboundary environmental pollution and promote sustainable development through environmental education and public participation. On a separate note, the ASCC Blueprint, guided by the

[23] Roadmap for an ASEAN Community 2009–2015, 2009, www.aseansec.org/publications/RoadmapASEANCommunity.pdf.

[24] Ibid.

[25] The main thrust of ASEAN's environmental strategies can be located in Section II, Part D of the ASCC Blueprint.

principles and purposes of the ASEAN Charter, builds on the ASEAN Security Community Plan of Action, the Vientiane Action Programme and other relevant decisions by various ASEAN sectoral bodies. The action-oriented document is in furtherance of the APSC's commitment to preserving peace and stability in the region, post-conflict peace-building and strengthening ASEAN humanitarian assistance, disaster management and emergency response.

5.4 ASEAN's Roadmap for the Millennium Development Goals (MDGs)

The primary goal of the ASCC is to build a people-centered ASEAN. The ASCC also focuses on narrowing the development gap among ASEAN member states. The Millennium Development Goals (MDGs) "mirror ASEAN's commitment to building a caring and sharing Community by 2015," for it sets out "goals and targets for improving wellbeing and reducing poverty in its broadest sense that are in line with the purposes of ASEAN."[26] ASEAN's commitment to accelerating the achievements of the MDGs has been reflected in a number of ASEAN documents issued by ASEAN leaders and ministers. Consequently, the ASEAN leaders called for the development and implementation of a Roadmap for the attainment of MDGs to serve as a framework at the 14th ASEAN Summit in 2009. The framework identified key areas

[26] ASEAN Roadmap for the Attainment of the Millennium Development Goals, August 5, 2011, www.asean.org/archive/documents/19th%20summit/MDG-Roadmap.pdf.

for collective actions namely, "advocacy and linkages, knowledge, resources, expertise, and regional cooperation and regional public goods."[27]

At the 2008 ASEAN Region Roundtable Meeting, the ASEAN Regional Center of Excellence on Millennium Development Goals was established to facilitate the integration process of ASEAN attainment of MDGs with ASEAN programs and initiatives so as to allow for a cohesive integration with the global community. At the establishment of the Center, the UN Secretary-General Ban Ki-Moon stated that "the Millennium Development Goals are no mere aspirations … they are commitments – sacred vows to the poorest, most vulnerable sections of humanity. Let us keep our promises. Let us build a world we can all be proud of."[28] At the 14th ASEAN Summit, ASEAN Leaders formally recognized[29] the Regional Center of Excellence as a platform to "share information, experience and best practices in the attainment of MDGs among ASEAN Member States."[30]

[27] Ibid., at p. 1.

[28] ASEAN Regional Center of Excellence on Millennium Development Goals, President's Message, www.ait.ac.th/news-and-events/2008/news-1/declaration-of-asean-regional-center-of-excellence-on-mdgs-at-ait/#.V01VtSZuk6Q.

[29] Joint Declaration on the Attainment of the Millennium Development Goals in ASEAN, Cha-am, Thailand, March 1, 2009, www.asean.org/asean/asean-summit/item/joint-declaration-on-the-attainment-of-the-millennium-development-goals-in-asean.

[30] Ibid.

5.5 Selected regional case studies

The following selection of case studies is chosen to illustrate the nature of transnational challenges that ASEAN has confronted in the last decade and how ASEAN has chosen to deal with them. These case studies not only illustrate intra-ASEAN cooperation, but also integration between ASEAN and the international community, including Dialogue Partners (e.g. EU,[31] United States, Australia, New Zealand, Canada and India), ASEAN Plus Three (China, Japan and Republic of South Korea), World Bank and the Asian Development Bank (ADB). The selection also demonstrates the vital role each ASEAN member state plays in the implementation of ASEAN's laws and policies in spite of self-serving politics, sovereignty and non-intervention. From a broader perspective, the issues presented here are common challenges that could affect the global community. Hence, they present an opportunity for ASEAN and the world to adopt an integrated, multifaceted approach in tackling these issues. There are always lessons to be learned. Environmental issues are not confined to a single isolated part of the world – instead the environment is largely *sans frontière*.

In reading the selections, consider if ASEAN is closer or further away from integration. Or, is each to be considered *sui generis*?

[31] See Asia-Europe Foundation, *Asia-Europe Environment Forum 2010, A Green Future: Asia and Europe Growing Sustainably*, Munich, Germany, September 1–3, 2010. This conference provided an opportunity to provide a platform for meaningful Asia-Europe exchanges via policy dialogue, cooperation and engagement between governments and private and civil society actors.

5.5.1 *Avian influenza*

In the last decade, there have been outbreaks of avian influenza (H5N1), severe acute respiratory syndrome (SARS) and swine influenza (H1N1) in the ASEAN region. For the purposes of this study, the focus is on avian influenza because the problems raised by other zoonotic diseases are similar.[32]

Avian influenza first surfaced in Hong Kong in 1997. Eighteen human cases were recorded, six of which were fatal. To eliminate the virus, the government depopulated all poultry markets in the country. In 2003, avian influenza resurfaced in Hong Kong. Only this time, it spread to other parts of Asia, including Cambodia, China, Indonesia, Japan, Lao PDR, Malaysia, Pakistan, Singapore, South Korea, Taiwan, Thailand and Vietnam. The disease then traveled to the Middle East, Europe, Central Asia, Russia and Africa. By April 12, 2006, it had infected 192 people worldwide, with

[32] K.-L. Koh, "Animal Health, Biodiversity Conservation and Sustainable Development: A Case Study of Avian Influenza," in Environmental Law Programme Newsletter, 2005/06, pp. 12–13; K.-L. Koh, "Public Health and Emerging Zoonotic Diseases," in International Development Law Organisation, *Globalizing Asia: Health Law and Governance Policy – Issues, Approaches and Gaps*, Bangkok, Thailand, April 16–18, 2012, www.researchgate.net/profile/Archie_Alexander/ publication/255717946_Globalizing_Asia_ Health_Law_Governance_and_Policy-Issues_and_Gaps!/links/ 02e7e52065e6d42551000000.pdf; K.-L. Koh and N. A. Robinson, "South-South Cooperation: Foundations for Sustainable Development" in S. Alam, S. Atapattu, C. G. Gonzalez and J. Razzaque (eds.), *International Environmental Law and the Global South* (New York: Cambridge University Press, 2015), pp. 553–71.

109 deaths. The world was at risk of a pandemic. Because the disease was transboundary, no one country could effectively tackle the problem, and cooperation was needed not only at the regional level but also globally.

In response to the avian influenza, the following institutional arrangements were made within ASEAN: the highest ASEAN sectoral bodies for human and animal health regional cooperation to prevent and control highly pathogenic avian influenza were the ASEAN Health Ministers Meeting and ASEAN Ministerial Meeting on Agriculture and Forestry. The subsidiary bodies were a Senior Officials Meeting on Health Development, ASEAN Expert Group on Communicable Diseases, ASEAN Sectoral Working Group on Livestock and ASEAN Highly Pathogenic Avian Influenza Task Force.

It was obvious why ASEAN acted with such energy. Not only was it faced with a pandemic threat, there were dire economic consequences. To that end, ASEAN collaborated with not only China, South Korea and Japan (ASEAN Plus 3), but also with international organizations such as the United Nations, World Health Organization, Food and Agriculture Organization and Office Internationale des Epizootics to draft legal frameworks and put in place legal and administrative systems. Among the goals of its cooperation with the international bodies were: to prevent and contain the virus; to reduce the risk to human and animal health; to strengthen the capacity of regional networks on surveillance; to respond at the regional and national levels in epidemiological surveillance and early warning in preparation for a pandemic. To

Table 5.1 Areas of cooperation among ASEAN member states

Disease surveillance	Thailand
Effective containment measures	Malaysia
Stamping out and vaccination policy	Indonesia
Diagnostic capabilities	Thailand
Establishment of disease-free zones	Malaysia
Information sharing	Singapore
Emergency preparedness plans	Malaysia
Public awareness	Philippines

that end, there were no less than ten ASEAN instruments on avian influenza.

The main areas of cooperation focused on activities that could be jointly implemented at a regional level to prevent transboundary and cross-border transmission. These activities included: establishment of strong networking in the areas of diseases surveillance; laboratory diagnosis; treatment and care; exchange of expertise for capacity building; and research and risk assessment. Table 5.1 outlines the eight areas of cooperation coordinated by member states during the outbreak.

In 2004, the ASEAN Health Ministers convened a number of meetings to discuss poultry disease control in response to the avian influenza and its role in international cooperation to effectively tackle emerging infectious diseases such as the avian influenza and SARS. ASEAN collaborated with Plus Three countries in responding to these diseases by, for example, sharing information and making use of existing mechanisms (i.e. ASEAN+3 Health Ministers hotline, ASEAN+3 List of Contact Points for Communicable Diseases and ASEAN Disease Surveillance website). The group also implemented a three-year ASEAN+3 Emerging Infectious Diseases Programme. Phase I of its Work Plan led to increased effectiveness of regional surveillance, early warning and response to emerging infectious diseases. The Plan also focused on strengthening capacities of countries to coordinate and manage effective implementation of the Emerging Infectious Diseases Programme in areas such as epidemiological surveillance, laboratory diagnostics, preparedness, early warning of outbreaks and rapid response to emerging infections.

On a wider scope, the Asia-Europe Foundation (ASEF) Public Health Network Programme[33] 2009–2013, funded by Japan, is one of the more recent initiatives in public health between Asia (including ASEAN) and Europe. Made up of Asian and European experts from public health authorities, NGOs and regional organizations, the Network serves as a bi-regional, multisectoral platform for enhanced collaboration on public health issues between Asia and Europe. It aims to strengthen capacity building and competence of frontline players in public health so as

[33] This Network demonstrates the integrated approach to transboundary public health – in this case, avian flu. The meeting was with the technical support of ASEAN, and funded by Japan. See Asia-Europe Foundation, *Expert Meeting on Regional Integration and Infectious Diseases*, Luxembourg, May 18–20, 2010, at p. 36, www.asef.org/index.php/pubs/asef-publications/2344-expert-meeting-on-regional-integration-and-infectious-diseases.

to better control potential outbreaks of disease. It also considers gaps in regional integration in combating infectious diseases.[34]

However, there were other areas that ASEAN could have considered and other organizations it could have cooperated with.

At the Eighth Meeting of the Conference of Parties to the Convention on Migratory Species of Wild Animals, the organization announced a new avian flu early warning system based on migratory bird maps. There were controversies surrounding migratory birds and a possible connection to avian influenza.[35] Today, scientists do think that migratory birds are a source of avian influenza. At the Eighth Meeting, the Assembly adopted the Resolution on Migratory Species and Highly Pathogenic Avian Influenza,[36] which called for integrated approaches at national and international levels to address animal-borne diseases by bringing together experts on ornithology, wildlife and wetland management and those traditionally responsible for public health and zoonosis.[37] The resolution also urged nations to police the illegal transport of captive birds and bird products, and drew attention

[34] Ibid., p. 2.

[35] See, for example, "Migratory Birds to Blame?" *The Straits Times*, January 29, 2004; "Experts Call Wild Birds Victims, Not Vectors," *New York Times – City Edition*, October 12, 2004.

[36] Convention on Migratory Species, Migratory Species and Highly Pathogenic Avian Influenza (Nairobi), UN Doc UNEP/CMS/Resolution 8.27 (2005), www.cms.int/avianflu/CMS_Resolution_8_27.pdf.

[37] Ibid.

to the importance of biosecurity measures and development of strategies that can limit the risk of disease transmission between wild and domestic animals, and humans.[38] The Food and Agriculture Organization of the United Nations and other organizations recommended good animal husbandry to control, monitor and vaccinate chickens in an effort to prevent future outbreaks. The Wildlife Conservation Society of the United States also laid down certain guidelines relative to the avian influenza outbreak.[39]

The challenges that ASEAN continues to face in light of the avian influenza call for a global platform for collaborative efforts on potential infectious diseases.[40] ASEAN cannot do it alone. Integration through law in cross-regional issues involves not only an intra-ASEAN but also an "ASEAN and the world" approach. This does not require the harmonization of laws, but rather an exchange of experiences to overcome differences and to identify priority areas. In this regard, the ASEF Public Health Network's recommendation, "integrating the 'One Health' into the policies, encompassing the animal, veterinary and human health sectors" is a viable one. To conclude, there was and is a need for ASEAN to cooperate with the world, and to adopt an

[38] Ibid.

[39] Wildlife Conservation Society, *Avian Influenza Guidelines Relative to the Outbreak in Asia* (New York: WCS, 2004); see also "The Manhattan Principles," as defined during the meeting, Building Interdisciplinary Bridges to Health in a "Globalised World" by WCS at the Rockefeller University, September 29, 2004, www.cdc.gov/onehealth/pdf/manhattan/twelve_manhattan_principles.pdf.

[40] Asia-Europe Foundation, *Expert Meeting on Regional Integration and Infectious Diseases*, p. 32.

integrated "ASEAN and the World" approach on a multilevel and multidisciplinary level to effectively tackle future outbreaks of avian influenza.

5.5.2 *"Haze"*

Transboundary pollution has been one of the common concerns of ASEAN since the 1990s, and when haze began to come from the member states, it became the focus of some ASEAN environmental instruments. In Indonesia, haze is the result of land-clearing fires for oil palm plantations; also, Indonesian farmers have practiced swidden (slash-and-burn) agriculture for years.[41] Some of the land-clearing is unauthorized, but often beyond the capacity of compliance and enforcement systems. Burning is the cheapest way to clear land, producing fires that can burn out of control. At times, the fires have been exacerbated by El Niño, spreading extensive air pollution to Kuala Lumpur and Singapore. Indonesia has considered these fires to be internal matters, and has declined assistance from ASEAN. Currently, it remains a challenge for ASEAN member states or the international community to implement measures to abate ongoing transboundary haze pollution. The situation from the 1990s persists to the present.[42] The worst haze episode occurred

[41] Asian Development Bank and Association of South East Asian Nations, *Fire, Smoke, and Haze: The ASEAN Response Strategy* (2001), pp. xiii–xvi.

[42] See "Haze Situation Worsens in 7 Areas in Malaysia," *The Straits Times*, June 16, 2012, www.straitstimes.com/Breaking+News/ANN/Story/STIStory_811641.html.

in June/July 2013, when Singapore's pollution standards index reached 400.[43] The haze also adversely impacted Malaysia. Haze also comes from Malaysia and other countries in the region that also practice swidden agriculture and land clearing for plantations.[44]

There are five environmental instruments directed at haze pollution: The Kuala Lumpur Accord on Environment and Development, 1990;[45] Singapore Resolution on Environment and Development, 1992;[46] ASEAN Cooperation Plan on Transboundary Pollution, 1995; the ASEAN Regional Haze Action Plan, 1997;[47] and the ASEAN Agreement on Transboundary Haze Pollution, 2002. The ASEAN Cooperation Plan on Transboundary Pollution, 1995, focuses on three areas: transboundary atmospheric pollution, transboundary movement of hazardous wastes and transboundary ship-borne pollution. To date, all ten member states have ratified the ASEAN Agreement on Transboundary Haze Pollution. Indonesia, where most of the haze originates due

43 https://sg.news.yahoo.com/year-in-review-2013–singapore-haze-levels-hit-psi-400–worst-in-16-years-044455629.html.

44 Haliza Abdul Rahman, *Haze Phenomenon in Malaysia – Domestic or Transboundary Factor?* Third International Journal Conference on Chemical Engineering and its Applications (ICCEA 13) September 28–29, 2013 Phuket (Thailand), www.isaet.org/images/extraimages/P913033.pdf.

45 The Kuala Lumpur Accord on Environment and Development, June 19, 1990, www.aseansec.org/6082.htm.

46 The ASEAN Declaration (Bangkok Declaration) Bangkok, August 8, 1967. See K.-L. Koh (compiler), *APCEL Document Series: Selected ASEAN Documents on the Environment* (APCEL, 1996), pp. ii–iv.

47 Haze Action Online, http://haze.asean.org/.

to the burning of peatlands and clearing of forests for agricultural practices, was the last to ratify the Agreement, in late 2014, though the country issued statements from 2011 that it might soon do so.[48] True to the *musyawara* and spirit of cooperation of ASEAN, despite Indonesia's non-ratification, neighboring countries have jointly provided aid to Indonesia during periods of forest fires.[49]

Since the recurrence of the haze in 2006, there has been a renewed concerted effort not only on the part of Indonesia, but other affected member states (Singapore, Malaysia, Brunei, Philippines and Thailand) and the global community to confront haze pollution. In spite of political, economic, socio-cultural and environmental problems, there seemed to be a breakthrough in early 2006 when an unexpected turn of events affected the solution of haze.[50] On October 20, 2006, Singapore tried to issue an ASEAN Statement at the United Nations to mobilize international support for a resolution on the haze issue. While the attempted call for international cooperation was not out of line under Article 2 of the Agreement on Transboundary

[48] "Indonesia to Ratify ASEAN Agreement on Transboundary Haze Pollution," *Antara News*, March 7, 2011, www.antaranews.com/en/news/68888/indonesia-to-ratify-asean-agreement-on-trans-boundary-haze-pollution.

[49] Indonesia–Singapore Collaboration to Deal with the Land and Forest Fires in Jambi Province, 2010, http://haze.asean.org/info/indo-sing.

[50] K.-L. Koh, "A Breakthrough in Solving the Indonesian Haze?" in S. Hart (ed.), *Shared Resources: Issues of Governance*, IUCN Environmental Law and Policy Paper No. 72, (Bonn: ICUN 2008), pp. 225–48, http://cmsdata.iucn.org/downloads/eplp_72.pdf.

Haze Pollution, Indonesia responded negatively to the attempt, believing it was an effort by its neighbor to shame the country at an international forum because there were already bilateral and regional arrangements in place.[51]

Perhaps because of the sensitivity of the issue, the ASEAN Charter lost an opportunity to address the principles of sovereignty and non-intervention in response to the Indonesian haze, even though the ASEAN Charter has enshrined these principles. Nonetheless, cooperation is through the NTS approach, which is ASEAN-centric and member-state-centric (the two 'centrics' include bottom-up and top-down approaches). The basis for submitting the issue to such an approach is human security, since air pollution from the Indonesian haze can cause long-term health problems in affected areas. Also, wild fires as environmental disasters fall within the scope of the ASEAN Agreement on Disaster Management and Emergency Response. Indeed, disaster response is covered in the APSC and the ASCC, but an issue can move from one pillar to another. It remains to be seen how political considerations will evolve to permit such an integrated approach.

From a different perspective, it can be noted that the Indonesian haze problem falls within the remit of the ASCC and not the APSC. Is this because it is a sensitive issue and, hence, less appropriate for an APSC approach?

[51] *The Straits Times*, November 4, 2006; see also, "ASEAN Needs Help to Tackle Haze: PM: International Expertise Needed to Help Nip Problem in the Bud," *The Straits Times*, November 6, 2006; "Embassy: Jakarta Prefers to Solve Haze within ASEAN," *The Straits Times*, November 9, 2006.

These two pillars are not mutually exclusive, and the haze issue could be assigned to either one. If, for example, the haze is exacerbated by the El Niño effect (as has occurred), the smoke can cover parts of Singapore, Malaysia and even the southern tip of Thailand and Philippines. When this happens, the health of the people is affected, and tourism and the economy also suffer. Haze pollution can also degrade ecosystems. From this perspective, the haze can entail "transboundary challenges" contemplated under APSC and attract the NTS approach; this approach would de facto sidestep the application of the principles of sovereignty and non-intervention.

Ultimately, it may be the response to new climate change challenges that stimulates measures to abate the use of fires to clear lands for agricultural purposes. ASEAN cooperation to study and agree upon regional best management practice measures to reduce emissions from deforestation and land degradation, and secure multilateral funding for such measures would be a plausible path to resolving the haze problems. This would be the more traditional ASEAN approach at quiet consensus building.

5.5.3 *Cyclone Nargis and Myanmar*

When Cyclone Nargis hit the delta region, ASEAN's role in providing humanitarian assistance and in mobilizing international assistance with dialogue partners, the UN and others illustrates how the "spirit" of ASEAN instruments (e.g. the ASEAN Agreement on Disaster Management and Emergency Response 2005, which was not then in force, see below) supports the *modus operandi* in Myanmar. It is important to note that the leadership of ASEAN's Secretary-General, Dr. Surin Pitsuwan and George Yeo, then Singapore's Foreign Minister were crucial in achieving a breakthrough in Myanmar's refusal of humanitarian aid.

When Cyclone Nargis caused widespread destruction of lives, property and the environment in Myanmar in May 2008, strong sovereignty and non-interference sentiments of the statehood threatened local human security. At the time, the APSC had not been formulated, nor were the ASEAN Charter and ASEAN Agreement on Disaster Management and Emergency Response 2005 in force. Instead, the Vientiane Action Plan was the relevant instrument in effect.

One of the reasons that contributed to Myanmar's initial decision to refuse humanitarian aid was fear of political implications in a country tightly controlled by the military. ASEAN assured Myanmar that assistance would not be politicized. Only then did Myanmar cooperate with ASEAN and allow access for humanitarian efforts to reach the disaster-struck areas. During this time, various government agencies and stakeholders provided necessary cooperation at various levels. The humanitarian assistance from ASEAN and others helped build confidence and bridged the gap for foreign rescue and humanitarian aid in Myanmar. The fact that the operation required the coordination of relevant government agencies at various levels, and with NGOs and civil society organizations, demonstrates the vital role of government and its cooperation in the NTS approach.

Cyclone Nargis was a natural disaster and not a human-induced environmental disaster. Nonetheless, its scope would now fall within the ASEAN Agreement on Disaster Management and Emergency Response.[52] Had the Agreement been in effect, ASEAN would have afforded Myanmar "comprehensive security" that required "enhanced" cooperation because the Agreement and ASEAN humanitarian assistance are within the bounds of the APSC Blueprint. Under the APSC Blueprint, ASEAN promises to "enhance joint effective and early response at the political and operational levels in activating the ASEAN disaster management arrangements to assist affected countries in the event of major disasters [and] to enhance civilian-military coordination in providing effective and timely response to major natural disasters,"[53] as agreed at the ASEAN Defence Ministers' Meeting.[54] The strengthening of disaster management by the military is significant because this is not the traditional role of the military. In fact, military involvement is sensitive from the political viewpoint, but Section II.B.6 of the APSC Blueprint provides that ASEAN will convene special meetings at leader or ministerial levels in the event of a crisis or an emergency that affects ASEAN, to develop

[52] Cyclone Nargis would fall within the scope of disaster under Article 1 of the Agreement. Disaster refers to "serious disruption of the function of a community or society causing widespread human, material, economic or environmental losses."

[53] Roadmap for an ASEAN Community 2009–2015.

[54] "ADMM Agrees to Strengthen ASEAN to Deal with Non-Traditional Security Threats," *People's Daily Online*, February 27, 2009, http://english.peopledaily.com.cn/90001/90777/90856/6602400.html.

arrangements to address such situation in a timely manner. In terms of integration, a classification under APSC that utilizes an NTS approach offers the cooperation of governments not just across ASEAN, but the rest of the world, especially when disaster and humanitarian management assistance are required.

5.5.4 *Thai floods and Typhoon Bopha and Typhoon Yolanda/Haiyan in the Philippines*

In 2011, severe flooding during the monsoon season caused widespread devastation in Thailand. The floods claimed more than 500 lives, disrupted the lives of 8.8 million others in more than 26 provinces and displaced more than 200,000 from their homes.[55] Many factories, including the Honda factory, were under water. Economic loss was significant.

The experience of Cyclone Nargis three years earlier allowed ASEAN to approach this disaster in a more efficient manner. On October 15, 2011, the ASEAN-Emergency Rapid Assessment Team (ASEAN-ERAT) was dispatched to Thailand to assess flood-affected areas and determine the basic and immediate needs of the affected population.[56]

[55] "Thailand Flooding 2011: Death Toll Above 600," *Huffington Post*, November 20, 2011, www.huffingtonpost.com/2011/11/20/thailand-flooding-2011-death-toll_n_1103930.html.

[56] "The ASEAN-Emergency Rapid Assessment Team Dispatched to Respond to Floods in Thailand," Jakarta, October 19, 2011, www.asean.org/news/asean-secretariat-news/item/the-asean-emergency-rapid-assessment-team-dispatched-to-respond-to-floods-in-thailand.

The ASEAN-ERAT, composed of experienced and trained individuals, is one of the response tools under the ASEAN Agreement on Disaster Management and Emergency Response.[57] This Agreement was created in response to the devastation caused by the tsunami in 2004, and spells out the importance of collaboration in the following areas: preparedness and response; partnership strategies; resource mobilization; outreach and mainstreaming; training and knowledge management; information management and communication technology.

It is important to note that the legal frameworks pertinent to disaster management (i.e. AADMER, which Thailand had ratified) were already in effect. By this time, ASEAN had adopted a robust approach toward disaster management in a changing climate regime. The ASEAN Committee on Disaster Management, which spearheaded the development of the AADMER Work Programme for the period 2010–2015, adopted an all-inclusive approach to put into action objectives from AADMER. The AADMER Work Programme consists of four strategic components: (1) disaster preparedness and response, (2) risk assessment, early warning and monitoring, (3) prevention and mitigation and (4) recovery. In addition, it also outlines several building blocks in order for these four components to be sustainably implemented, such as training, knowledge management, strengthening and forming new

[57] ASEAN Agreement on Disaster Management and Emergency Response, Vientiane, July 26, 2005, www.asean.org/communities/asean-socio-cultural-community/item/the-asean-agreement-on-disaster-management-and-emergency-response.

partnerships, and use of information and communications technologies.[58]

Again, the "whole of ASEAN" approach was necessary in response to the crisis in Thailand. ASEAN has since signed a memorandum of understanding with the UN to strengthen its disaster management and intensify its regional and international cooperation.[59] With the frequency of natural and human-induced disasters around the world, worldwide cooperation is emerging to deal with disaster management.

The approach was reprised when Typhoon Bopha hit the Mindanao regions in the Philippines on December 3, 2012. More than five million people were affected, 906 were dead, 2,660 were injured and 932 were missing. The ASEAN Coordinating Center for Humanitarian Assistance on Disaster Management (AHA Center) deployed the ASEAN-ERAT to assess needs and to quickly provide necessary aid to the disaster-affected areas.[60] Member states also sent aid and deployed response teams to assist in planning

[58] ACDM Joint Statement on the Occasion of the 4th Ministerial Conference for Disaster Risk Reduction, Incheon, Republic of Korea, October 25–28, 2010, www.aseansec.org/25407.htm.

[59] Joint Declaration on Comprehensive Partnership between the Association of Southeast Asian Nations and the United States, Bali, November 19, 2011, www.aseansec.org/documents/19th%20summit/UN-JD.pdf.

[60] "Association of Southeast Asian Nations, ASEAN Supports the Typhoon Affected Communities in The Philippines," www.asean.org/news/asean-secretariat-news/item/asean-supports-the-typhoon-affected-communities-in-the-philippines.

and preparation in these areas. Following the disaster, the AHA Center launched a Disaster Emergency Logistics System for ASEAN to "provide rapid delivery of relief items in times of disaster emergencies."[61] Typhoon Bopha paled into significance against Typhoon Haiyan/Yolanda, which ravaged the Philippines on November 8, 2013, with Leyte and Samar being hardest hit.[62] Soon after the occurrence, the United Nations reported that over eleven million people were affected, in terms of loss of lives (estimated as high as 10,000 and more were to be subsequently reported), property and much else besides. Haiyan was likened to Hurricane Katrina.[63]

ASEAN (and the world) *has* awakened to the fact that many disasters in Asia (such as the tsunami of 2004) need a "whole-of-the-world" approach. Indeed, AADMER was

[61] Ibid.

[62] www.youtube.com/watch?v=4wrgrJwYdy8. See K.-L.Koh and R. L. Eisma-Osorio, "The Role of ASEAN in Disaster Management: Legal Framework and Case Study of Typhoon Haiyan/Yolanda," in K.-L. Koh, I. Kelman, R. Kubugi and R. L. Eisma-Osorio (eds.), *Adaptation to Climate Change: ASEAN and Comparative Experiences* (World Scientific,2015), Chapter 18; see also *Typhoon Yolanda Book, 'Y' (It Happened)* and *The ASEAN Book, Weathering the Perfect Storm* – www.asean.org/news/asean-secretariat-news/item/statement-of-the-secretary-general-of-asean-for-the-launching-of-typhoon-yolanda-book-y-it-happened-and-asean-book-weathering-the-perfect-storm.

[63] www.irinnews.org/report/84423/global, "Disaster Risk Increasing: Exacerbated by Climate Change - Report." The first UN Global Assessment Report on Disaster Reduction launched the report on May 17, 2009: "If climate change added to these disaster risk patterns, it will be quite a catastrophic picture."

formulated after the 2004 Asian tsunami hit a number of ASEAN member states causing untold damage in terms of lives, property and much more. ASEAN was then "non-existent" at the scene as it had only a very rudimentary soft law disaster framework, the ASEAN Declaration on Mutual Assistance on Natural Disasters 1976, which only dealt with disaster warnings, exchange of information and dissemination of medical supplies. The Asian tsunami was a clarion call at the highest level of ASEAN to draft AADMER, which is a hard law treaty. The tsunami also inspired a World Conference on Disaster Reduction in January 2005 in Hyogo, Japan, which adopted the Hyogo Declaration and the Hyogo Framework for Action. The Hyogo Framework stressed the need to strengthen and develop coordinated regional approaches for effective disaster response.

The kinds of disaster risk are numerous. Just to mention some direct damage and impacts: death, property and infrastructure destruction. As for "indirect" impacts, these include pollution, disease, food and water shortages, looting, raping, and so on. What kinds of emergency response are needed? What governance system should be put in place, what kinds of responsibilities arise from donors and parties in terms of, for example, relief supplies where there are delays due to clearance or simply an overwhelming amount of goods that choke up clearance procedures causing delays – who pays for demurrage, the donor or the disaster party? What are the issues in the aftermath of the disaster? Recovery can be a long process and bring with it a different set of problems, not to mention funding issues. These are some of a litany of woes of disaster management that can confront ASEAN or any donor.

Haiyan provided an opportunity for ASEAN to enhance its cooperation with its member states and ASEAN has since scaled up its disaster management operations.

5.5.5 *Wildlife crimes*

As discussed in Chapter 4, illegal trade in wildlife has been on the rise at a local and national level.[64] Traders of this illicit activity range from small players to huge syndicates; illegal

[64] See ASEAN Wildlife Enforcement Network. We would like to thank Brian Gonzales, USAID-ARREST Program Lead Liaison Officer of ASEAN-WEN; Steven Galster, Chief of Party of the USAID-ARREST Program/FREELAND Foundation; and John Webb, former Assistant Chief for their inputs in this section and for providing some important materials. See also Terms of Reference (TOR) of the ASEAN Wildlife Enforcement Network (2006); ASEAN Socio-Cultural Community Blueprint (ASCC 2009–2015); ASEAN Regional Action Plan on Trade in CITES Wild Fauna and Flora (2011–2015); Strategic Plan of Action (SPA) on ASEAN Cooperation in CITES (2011–2015); Initiative for ASEAN Integration Strategic Framework and Work Plan 2 (2009–2015); Strategic Schedule for ASEAN Economic Community (2009–2015). See also K.-L. Koh, "Transnational Illegal Wildlife Trade Plus (TIWT+): 'Transnational Crimes and Transboundary Challenges' under the 'ASEAN Political-Security Community Blueprint (APSC)'," 3rd Edition, ASEANAOL Bulletin, 3rd Edition, 2014, 28–34. See EAS Declaration on Combating Wildlife Trafficking, www.mofa.go.jp/mofaj/files/000059731.pdf; the London Declaration on the Illegal Wildlife Trade, February 13, 2014, www.gov.uk/government/uploads/system/uploads/attachment_data/file/281289/london-wildlife-conference-declaration-140213.pdf; Follow up Conference on the London Declaration on Illegal Wildlife Trade in Kasane, Botswana, March 23–25, 2015, www.ambafrance-bw.org/Biodiversity-Kasane-Conference-on.

trade generates hundreds of millions of dollars annually. ASEAN has not yet attempted to categorize cross-border trade in wildlife plants and animals as transnational crimes pursuant to Section II B.4 of the APSC Blueprint that lists drugs and human trafficking, money laundering and terrorism as transnational crimes. There are countries that believe sovereignty and non-intervention is of relevance because of territorial integrity. However, these countries (including some ASEAN member states) do not realize the disastrous environmental and criminal consequences brought on by illegal wildlife trade. Illegal wildlife trade endangers species, threatens biological diversity and human health, and is coming to be regarded as "ecocide."[65] Given the severity of wildlife crime and the extinction of species, it is not implausible to consider that ASEAN could list these crimes under the APSC.

Increased urgency to combat illegal wildlife trade has attracted the attention of the United Nations and other countries. The Commission on Crime Prevention and Criminal Justice of the United Nations Economic and Social Council[66] called for international cooperation in preventing

[65] K. Kangaspunta, "Who Commits Eco-crimes, Freedom From Fear," www.freedomfromfearmagazine.org/index.php?option=com_content&view=article&id=225:who-commits-eco-crimes&catid=49:issue-6&Itemid=186; see also UNODC, "Organized Crime and Drug Trafficking Major Threats to International Security," www.unodc.org/unodc/en/frontpage/2011/November/organized-crime-and-drug-trafficking-major-threats-to-international-peace-and-security.html; and Patrick Curry, "Defending Humanities in a Time of Ecocide," www.youtube.com/watch?v=9a1bx8Pott4.

[66] See UNODC, *Crime-related Resolutions and Decisions*, www.unodc.org/unodc/en/commissions/CCPCJ/05-resolutions-.html.

and combating illicit transnational trafficking in forest products, including timber, wildlife and other forest biological resources. In his address to the UN Security Council on November 23, 2011, Mr. Fedotov, head of UN Office of Drugs and Crime, pointed out that transnational organized crimes and drug trafficking together with wildlife transactions are undermining security in many regions, and evolving into major threats to political and social stability, the rule of law, human rights and economic development. He noted that his Office is:

> using partnerships with a number of United Nations entities such as the World Health Organization, the Office of the United Nations High Commissioner for Refugees, the Department of Peacekeeping Operations, the Department of Political Affairs, UNAIDS and the World Bank, among others, to create a multidisciplinary response in such areas as … illegal trade in small arms, corruption, illicit money flows, human trafficking and *wildlife crime*.[67]

It is noteworthy that the U.S. Congressional Research Service Report for Congress on "International Illegal Trade in Wildlife: Threats and U.S. Policy" (2008) cataloged human and wildlife risks resulting from the illegal trade in wildlife.

[67] I. Davison, "Eco-Crimes are Crimes Against Humanity," *NZHerald*, September 6, 2011, www.nzherald.co.nz/nz/news/article.cfm?c_id=1&objectid=10749842; see also *International Cooperation in Preventing and Combating Illicit International Trafficking in Forest Products, Including Timber, Wildlife and Other Forest Biological Resources*, Report of the Executive Director, 2008, UNESOC, E/CN.15/2008/9.

The service report points out that illegal transnational wildlife trafficking has led to population collapse and the extinction of certain species. Illegal logging and wildlife trafficking are inextricably linked as expansions into virgin forests open a network of roads subsequently used to support poaching and trade in forest species. As an example of this threat, the mileage on roads primarily to facilitate logging in the United States is three or four times higher than the total mileage on interstate highways.

Illegal wildlife trafficking is a problem across the entire ASEAN region. Since the term "ecocide" has entered the world of environmental terminology,[68] it might be asked whether ASEAN would move toward classifying "ecocide" as a crime. All ASEAN member states have ratified the Convention on International Trade in Endangered Species (CITES),[69] but national laws pursuant to CITES implementation are mostly outdated and/or inadequate. Weak implementation of CITES by member states is compounded by its individual failure to elevate such crimes to an NTS issue pursuant to APSC, thus bringing illegal wildlife trade to the same level of seriousness as transnational crimes. Current enforcement in member states is sectoral; each agency in member states addresses CITES issues within a narrow compartmentalized authority with virtually no coordination from other relevant agencies such as customs, police, military, transport,

68 "Ecocide: Destruction of the natural environment, especially when willfully done." Oxford Dictionaries Online 2012, http://oxforddictionaries.com/definition/ecocide?region=us.

69 Convention on International Trade in Endangered Species of Wild Fauna and Flora, www.cites.org.

foreign affairs departments, the private sector, NGOs or civil society organizations. Enforcement often results in mere seizure and forfeiture of contraband wildlife, and penalties are light compared to the unlawful profits of illegal wildlife trafficking. In such an enforcement situation, there is no deterrence. A stricter criminal law regime is needed in each state across the entire ASEAN region.

Combating wildlife crime is a highly visible way to re-establish and bolster the rule of law in many ASEAN states. Corruption and weak systems of law administration and enforcement affect more than the environmental sphere, but the global pressure through CITES stimulates immediate and effective measures to restore honesty in government. Without the rule of law, ASEAN will not realize its objectives of sustainable development. Here, then, is a concrete case where the question of integration through law can be tested. CITES enforcement is growing rapidly. It remains to be seen how ASEAN will collaborate to attain common standards of honest administration of its national customs inspections, coupled with prosecutions and effective criminal court proceedings.

If illegal trade in wildlife plants and animals were to be categorized as transnational crimes pursuant to APSC, enforcement procedures might be different. There is a growing recognition of the seriousness in illegal wildlife trade and its relation to international and national security in ASEAN and the rest of the world. Enforcement by ASEAN and the international community needs a unified, integrated approach because no one country or region can deal with the issue alone.

At the Thirteenth Conference of the Parties to CITES in October 2004, in Bangkok, it was noted that illegal trade in endangered species needed more cooperation among member countries.[70] Following the Conference, ASEAN issued the "ASEAN Statement on CITES," highlighting six key areas of cooperation, including promoting regional cooperation for effective enforcement and strengthening borders in key regions.[71] Subsequently, the ASEAN Regional Action Plan on Trade in Wild Fauna and Flora 2005–2010[72] was launched at the Special Meeting of the ASEAN Ministers Responsible for the Implementation of CITES in December 2005. The Regional Action Plan has since been replaced by the Strategic Plan of Action on ASEAN Cooperation in CITES (2011–2015).

Pursuant to the Regional Action Plan, the ASEAN Wildlife Enforcement Network[73] (ASEAN-WEN) was established to promote networking among enforcement authorities in ASEAN and the world to combat the illegal trade in wildlife. The ASEAN-WEN Program Coordination Unit was set up to facilitate and coordinate

[70] ASEAN Statement on CITES on the Occasion of the Thirteenth Conference of the Parties to CITES, Bangkok, October 11, 2004, www.aseansec.org/16470.htm. See also J. Lin, "Tackling Southeast Asia's Illegal Wildlife Trade," in C. L. Lim (ed.), *Singapore Year Book of International Law* (Commonwealth Legal Information Institute, 2005) at pp. 191–208.

[71] Ibid.

[72] ASEAN Regional Action Plan on Trade in Wild Fauna and Flora 2005–2010, Jakarta, May 3, 2005, www.aseansec.org/17753.pdf.

[73] See ASEAN Wildlife Enforcement Network.

technical support for ASEAN-WEN at the regional and global levels, including intelligence sharing, reviewing weak laws and coordinating enforcement action.[74] Its networks include relevant governmental, intergovernmental and non-governmental organizations in ASEAN and non-ASEAN countries. ASEAN-WEN is also assisted by Freeland Foundation's Asia's Regional Response to Endangered Species Trafficking (ARREST) Program, a USAID-funded private-public partnership program, which originally led the U.S. Support Program to ASEAN-WEN from 2006 to 2010.[75] The ARREST Program is in support of the official ASEAN-U.S. Enhanced Partnership, officially approved by the Governments of ASEAN and the United States.[76] ASEAN-WEN has also developed links with the World Wildlife Fund, United Nations Office on Drugs and Crime (UNODC), International Consortium on Combating Wildlife Crime, World Bank, INTERPOL, the World Customs Union, the CITES Secretariat, TRAFFIC and WildAid, as well as ASEAN customs, police,

[74] See, for example, "Asian Nations Launch Regional Plan to Smash Wildlife Smuggling Rings," *Agence France-Presse*, November 11, 2004, www.aseansec.org/afp/75p.htm; and ASEAN Statement on Launching of the ASEAN Wildlife Law Enforcement Network, Bangkok, December 1, 2005, www.aseansec.org/17933.htm.

[75] USAID/ASIA – Asia's Regional Response to Endangered Species Trafficking (ARREST).

[76] FREELAND, "Asia's Regional Response to Endangered Species Trafficking," http://freeland.org/eng/wildlife-trafficking/what-we-do/arrest.

prosecutors, specialized governmental wildlife law enforcement organizations, other relevant national law enforcement agencies[77] and others to eradicate wildlife crime and the syndicates involved. ASEAN-WEN also actively engages with civil society by raising awareness of issues of legality and sustainability.[78] ASEAN-WEN together with Freeland's ARREST Program[79] has recently entered into a partnership with the Asia-Pacific Centre for Environmental Law (APCEL)[80] at the National University of Singapore[81] to develop an ASEAN Legal Studies and Support Program for Nature Protection to improve governmental and civil

[77] The latest is the China and ASEAN-WEN Network (following a meeting on Wildlife Enforcement Cooperation and CITES Matters from June 18–19, 2012, Nanning, China). A "Statement of Cooperation" was issued on technical consultation to strengthen cooperation on wildlife enforcement. This will pave the way for an official agreement under the ASEAN+ 3 framework.

[78] ASEAN Action Plan on Wildlife Trade, Indian Jungles, May 26, 2005, www.indianjungles.com/280505.htm.

[79] See Asia's Regional Response to Endangered Species Trafficking.

[80] Law Faculty, National University of Singapore, Asia Pacific Centre for Environmental Law (APCEL), http://law.nus.edu.sg/apcel/.

[81] A seminar was held on May 30, 2012, at the Law Faculty, National University of Singapore *on Strengthening ASEAN Wildlife Enforcement Network (ASEAN-WEN) through Public-Private Partnerships in Legal Cooperation*. This was followed by an ASEAN-WEN Regional Stakeholders Policy Workshop hosted by the Law Faculty's APCEL, December 8–10, 2014. See K.-L. Koh, "Transnational Illegal Wildlife Trade Plus (TIWT+) and 'Transnational Crimes and Transboundary Challenges' Under the 'ASEAN Political - Security Community' Blueprint (APSC)," in ASEANAPOL Bulletin, 3rd edn, 2014, 28–34; Kuala Lumpur Declaration in Combating Transnational Crime.

society awareness and utilization of legal instruments to prevent and prosecute eco-crime or "transnational crimes" under APSC.[82]

Wildlife crimes are now on the agendas for ASEAN Ministerial Meetings on Transnational Crimes and also Senior Officials Meetings on Transnational Crimes. As ASEAN moves toward the realization of an ASEAN community and also toward a global community, enhanced cooperation in combating transnational crimes is an important part of establishing security and enabling prosperity in the region. The support that is now given to ASEAN-WEN by the ministerial and senior officials meetings on transnational crime will hopefully lead ASEAN to review the laws relating to wildlife crime including customs and quarantine laws and CITES laws to allow for effective enforcement. It is hoped that when appropriate situations arises, ASEAN and member states will not hesitate to invoke Section II B.4 of APSC to recognize illegal wildlife trade as transnational crimes.

The APSC notion of transnational crimes is aligned with the definition of the UN on transnational crimes "as offences whose inception, prevention and/or direct or

[82] T. B. van Solinge, "Eco-Crime: The Tropical Timber Trade," in D. Siegel and H. Nelen (eds.), *Organized Crime: Culture, Markets and Policies* (Springer, 2008). As a legal category, eco-crime has been defined as "an unauthorized act or omission that violates the law and is therefore subject to criminal prosecution and criminal sanction": E. McLaughlin and J. Muncie, *The Sage Dictionary of Criminology*, 2nd edn. (Sage Publications, 2005).

indirect effects involved more than one country."[83] The UN has identified eighteen different categories of transnational crime. Among these are money laundering, terrorist activities, illicit traffic in arms, *environmental crime*, trafficking in persons, illicit drug trafficking, corruption and bribery of public officials and other offences committed by organized criminal groups. The UN also recognizes that such crimes impact on international and national security.[84] This list is in line with those listed in the APSC.

An "ASEAN-and-the-world" integrated approach, similar to the one adopted in response to the avian influenza would strengthen the enforcement of not only illegal wildlife trade, but also all transnational crimes connected with it. In the context of wildlife trade within ASEAN, it could lead to gradual harmonization of some aspects of the laws relating to such trade, or at least lead to enhanced cooperation with INTERPOL and other partners playing an active role.

The integrative strategy should include deployment of multiagency national police with full police powers, proactive investigative techniques (e.g. undercover), covert investigations and controlled deliveries and detection, preservation, and use of electronic evidence, and aggressive national prosecution with multifaceted remedies, imprisonment, fines, forfeitures of instrumentalities, disgorgement of

[83] Definition reproduced in G. Mueller, 'Transnational Crime: Definitions and Concepts," in P. Williams and D. Vlassis (eds.), *Combating Transnational Crime*, a Special Issue of *Transnational Organized Crime*, 4(3/4), (Autumn/Winter 1998), p. 18.

[84] List reprinted in Mueller, "Transnational Crime: Definitions and Concepts," p. 14.

illegal proceeds, and reparations for environmental harm. Transnational organized crime profiting from illegal wildlife trafficking should face the same challenges and risks as when committing other transnational crimes under APSC. Until this happens transnational eco-crime will remain a multi-billion-dollar business plundering the world's natural resources with impunity, with no greater risk than stealing the contents of an open, unguarded safe.

5.5.6 ASEAN's strategic transnational water action plan

At the 20th ASEAN Summit held in 2012 in Cambodia, ASEAN leaders agreed to "continue to reinforce all efforts to promote sustainable management of water resources to ensure the interest of all the peoples of ASEAN, including those people along the Mekong River and riparian countries."[85]

The ASEAN Strategic Plan of Action on Water Resources Management[86] (AWRM) provides useful guidance for member states to develop integrated water management as part of their obligations under international instruments such as Agenda 21, the Convention on Biological

[85] Phnom Penh Declaration on ASEAN: One Community, One Destiny, Phnom Penh, April 3, 2012, www.aseansec.org/documents/pp_declaration_3%20April_FINAL.pdf.

[86] ASEAN Strategic Plan of Action on Water Resources Management 2005, http://environment.asean.org/files/ASEAN%20Strategic%20Plan%20of%20Action%20on%20Water%20Resources%20Management.pdf.

Diversity and the Convention on Wetlands of International Importance especially as Waterfowl Habitat. Management of water resources includes water accessibility, water quality, adequacy of supply of water and environmental flows, reasonable pricing to achieve equity and water for ecosystem services, mitigation of water-related hazards, and water sanitation; these are basics for maintaining human physical and mental health and the right to human life and dignity.[87] This case study provides an illustration of the global role of ASEAN in facilitating implementation of principles on water from Chapter 18 of Agenda 21[88] and also Rio+20.[89]

The AWRM comes within the ambit of the ASEAN Working Group on Water Resources Management. While the AWRM is only a framework document i.e. soft law, its guidelines are essential to the development of integrated water resource management and water sustainability in the region. The vision and mission statements of AWRM capture some of the important elements found in global water policies.

[87] K.-L. Koh, "ASEAN Strategic Plan of Action on Water Resources Management, 2005: How Sustainable and the Way Forward: A Commentary," in IUCN Academy of Environmental Law, *Academy's Ninth Annual Colloquium, Water and the Law: Towards Sustainability*, South Africa July 3–7, 2011.

[88] UNEP, *Protection of the Quality and Supply of Freshwater Resources: Application of Integrated Approaches to the Development, Management and Use of Water Resources*, www.earthsummit2002.org/ic/freshwater/reschapt18.html.

[89] Rio+20 United Nations Conference on Sustainable Development (Rio de Janeiro) UN Doc A/CONF.216/L.1 (2012), The Future We Want, 66/288,www.un.org/ga/search/view_doc.asp?symbol=A/RES/66/288&Lang=E.

In addition, the AWRM promotes an integrated approach forwarded by Southeast Asia's *Vision for Water in the 21st Century*: "the attainment of sustainability of water resources to ensure sufficient water quantity of acceptable quality to meet the needs of Southeast Asia in terms of health, food security, economy and environment."[90] Integration would involve mainstreaming policies at lateral and vertical levels, and across sectors such as land use planning and ecological systems.

One of the crucial elements for water sustainability is governance, as affirmed in the second principle of AWRM, Section 6, which seeks to include "an appropriate governance framework." The essentials of good governance include good policies, planning and awareness. The Mekong River Basin Agreement is an example of multilevel water governance in ASEAN.

As a regional organization, ASEAN could harmonize regional integration by bringing together cohesive water policies and best practices from the international and regional community. It could incorporate latest issues (such as changes brought on by climate change) and adopt an ecological approach toward water. In this respect, non-natural freshwater resources are also important, such as Singapore's NEWater, discussed in Chapter 4.

The impact of climate change has exerted great pressure on water resources in ASEAN. At the 15th

[90] Global Water Partnership, *Our Vision for Water in the 21st Century*, www.gwp.org/Global/The%20Challenge/Resource%20material/FFA%20regional%20summary%20SEA.pdf.

ASEAN Summit, held in Thailand in 2009, ASEAN leaders addressed the need for ASEAN to further develop integrated, people-oriented approaches for water resources management and exchange knowledge in adapting to water resources problems, particularly water-related disaster management, trans-basin and coastal water resources, to find a balance between the need for food production and sustainability of natural resources. The Summit also pointed out the inclusion of an integrated coastal and ocean management approach to prepare for and adapt to the adverse effects of climate change, as reflected in the Manado Ocean Declaration, 2009.[91] ASEAN's realization of the impact of climate change and other factors (such as population growth) on food security has spawned a number of policies, programs, plans and strategies. The agriculture-dependent economies of ASEAN member states most affected by the impact of climate change on agriculture are Indonesia, the Philippines, Thailand and Vietnam.

In comparison, the Convention on Biological Diversity (CBD) COP 17 Decision VII/4 of 2007[92] highlighted the importance of inland water ecosystems on biodiversity. The CBD's inland waters program promotes the ecosystem approach, including integrated watershed management, as the best way to reconcile competing demands for dwindling supplies of inland waters. It is essential that

[91] See www.cep.unep.org/news-and-events/manado-ocean-declaration/view.

[92] Convention on Biological Diversity, Conference of the Parties Decision VII/11 on Ecosystem Approach, www.cbd.int/decision/cop/?id=7748.

the maintenance of biodiversity is seen as a critical demand for freshwater use, and is managed in coordination with other demands. The ecosystem approach provides a framework for the *integrated* management of land, water and living resources. Its application could facilitate the formulation of climate change mitigation and adaptation projects that also contribute to biodiversity conservation and sustainable use at the national level.

On July 28, 2010, nine of the ten ASEAN member states (the Philippines was "absent") joined 122 delegates to vote in favor of adopting the UN General Assembly Resolution on the human right to water and sanitation. The Resolution could have a potential impact on AWRM. If ASEAN were to include the right to water and sanitation in its terms of reference for the ASEAN Intergovernmental Commission on Human Rights (AICHR) it would have to work out the scope of obligations imposed on governments by including the protection of water resources, conservation and other principles (water as an economic and public good, equity in water and access to justice) under the right to water.

To conclude, it is not clear how many member states have aligned their water law policies and governance framework with the AWRM to date. The one-size-fits-all approach does not always make for integration in the region.

Chapter 6

ASEAN and climate disruption

> Climate change may be one issue in which bottom-up demands and initiatives could force reluctant governments to act. In any case, the problem cannot be solved unless each one of us is willing to take ownership of the problem and do our little bit to reduce our carbon footprint. Therefore, we should not allow the elusive post-Kyoto agreement to stop us from doing the right thing. The future of the Earth and of human civilization depends upon each of us.
>
> Ambassador and Professor Tommy Koh[1]

Climate disruption will complicate ASEAN's efforts to build sustainable development across all its member states. The impacts will either be a force for strengthening environmental safeguards needed to cope with climate change and thus enhance legal integration through ASEAN, or the disruptions will have a disintegration effect, reducing states to reliance on their own internal systems, however lacking they may be.[2] The case studies in Chapter 5 suggest that it

[1] Keynote Speech, "Workshop on Crucial Issues in Climate Change and the Kyoto Protocol: Asia and the World," organized by the Asia-Pacific Centre for Environmental Law (APCEL), August 30, 2007, National University of Singapore.

[2] K.-L. Koh and L. Bhullar, "ASEAN and Climate Change: The Singapore Declaration on Climate Change, Energy and the Environment,

will be through cooperation and greater integration that the region can best cope. Whether integration through law (ITL) will in fact advance remains to be seen. The dynamics affecting decisions about ITL in the context of responding to climate change can be examined through examining how climate change will affect natural biological resources of Southeast Asia.

According to the Intergovernmental Panel on Climate Change,[3] the impacts of climate change for biodiversity resources in the ASEAN region are projected to be serious. Climate change will exacerbate the many factors that are already endangering biodiversity in the region. A significant number of the region's population remains in poverty, many subsisting mainly on the uninterrupted use of biological natural resources, the losses of which are increasing progressively.[4] Climate change impacts buttress one another: climate change exacerbates poverty and accelerates biodiversity loss; poverty sequentially compels the poor to exploit the environment

2007 and Beyond," in W. Scholtz and J. Verschuuren, *Regional Environmental Law. Transregional Comparative Lessons in Pursuit of Sustainable Development* (Edward Elgar: 2015), Chapter 10. See also International Bar Association, *Achieving Justice and Human Rights in an Era of Climate Disruption*, July 2014, www.ibanet.org/PresidentialTaskForceClimateChangeJustice2014Report.aspx.

[3] Fourth Assessment Report of the Intergovernmental Panel on Climate Change, http://chm.aseanbiodiversity.org/index.php?option=com_content&view=article&id=139&Itemid=225.

[4] See, for example, L. Elliott and M. Caballero-Anthony, *Human Security and Climate Change in Southeast Asia: Managing Risk and Resilience* (Routledge 2013).

unsustainably. Degraded environments, in return, intensify poverty and hasten climate change. The bottom line is that if deforestation in the region continues at its current rate, Southeast Asia stands to lose up to three-quarters of its forests and up to 42 percent of its biodiversity by 2100.

How each ASEAN member state responds to the challenges of climate change will measure the success or failure of its socio-economic development. Previously agreed objectives for sustainable development must be recast in light of the changing physical conditions across Southeast Asia. ASEAN can foster collaboration among its member states to prepare each for adapting to the new environmental conditions. ASEAN's working groups and its consultative meetings and exchanges of information help ensure that all governments at least share the same awareness of the looming problems. In the immediate future, ASEAN will need to scale up regional cooperation to cope with the effects of the pervasive shifts in weather patterns, greatly disruptive storms and sea-level rise along the extensive coastlines. To avert trends that exacerbate climate change, such as the release of greenhouse gases locked in peat and wetlands, ASEAN will need to support measures to reduce emissions from degradation of these lands. Sometimes short-term and longer-term objectives can coincide, as in combating regional haze by working to prevent fires in peatlands and forests, and restoring wetlands by moving oil palm plantations from peat soils to other locations,[5] thereby enabling restoration of peat wetlands.

[5] These proposals are debated under the UN Framework Convention on Climate Change as "land use, land use change, and forestry" (or LULUCF). Since deforestation has produced nearly 90 percent

In other contexts, new dimensions of planning for sustainable urban resettlement can remove people from low-lying coastal areas to new "eco-cities" situated in safer interior locations.

Neither ASEAN nor its member states are staffed adequately to seize such opportunities for establishing new sustainable development patterns or to cope with the adverse impacts that undermine existing "business as usual" patterns of development. ASEAN is not unique in this respect; all regions have yet to make the shift to a new paradigm. Peter Bakker, president of the World Business Council for Sustainable Development and its 200 member companies, has described this global challenge. At the Rio+20 Conference on Sustainable Development in June 2012, he acknowledged that huge gains have been made:

> to decouple economic growth, human development, and well-being from negative environmental and social impacts … But this hard-won progress has been overwhelmed by the sheer amount of fossil fuels, materials, and wastes flowing through the world economy

of greenhouse gas emissions associated with LULUCF since 1850, proposals have emerged on "Reducing Emissions from Deforestation and Degradation" (REDD). The UN Food and Agricultural Organization reports that Southeast Asia experiences the most rapid deforestation of any region. Because marketing timber products as commodities and clearing forests for conversion to farming and cash crop plantations is lucrative, the ASEAN governments have been reluctant to address deforestation and land use changes. See generally C. Streck, "Protecting Forests to Mitigate Global Climate Change," in K.-L. Koh, L.-H. Lye and J. Lin (eds.), *Crucial Issues in Climate Change and the Kyoto Protocol – Asia and the World* (World Scientific Press, 2010), p. 559.

> … Without significant cuts in our greenhouse-gas emissions soon, we face a rise in global temperatures of five degrees Celsius that is predicted to cause massive flooding in large cities like London and New York, and severe water shortages in China and India.[6]

Cities in the Philippines and across Indochina already have experienced the first of these floods.

In 2012 the scientific journal *Nature* published a series of review analyses of the trends that make manifest the shift of Earth from its patterns of gradual changes to a forced new planetary state.[7] The biosphere is being degraded in ways and at scales and rates unprecedented in human history. Across ASEAN, socio-economic conditions will be disrupted further. Among the local effects states must anticipate will be losses of ecosystem services that human settlements depend upon, droughts and floods as unpredictable events, the collapse of many marine fish species, the loss of vast forest areas and the regional loss of agricultural lands, drastic redistributions of species and increasing numbers of species extinctions, extensive heat and humidity and a lack of capacity to generate electricity as human demand overwhelms supply. These impacts will be exacerbated by a significant migration of people, away from the coastal areas eroded by higher sea levels and storm surges and away from places where storms or other effects have rendered human settlements no longer habitable. Suffice it to say, governments will be increasingly

[6] P. Bakker, "Sustainability as a Logistics Challenge," *International Herald Tribune*, June 20, 2012, p. 16.

[7] Vol. 486, no. 7401 (June 7, 2012).

hard pressed to provide a rapidly growing ASEAN urban population with food, jobs, education, water and homes. It has not gone unnoticed that such disruptive effects of climate change can give rise to threats to peace and security,[8] the core concerns that gave rise to the impetus to establish ASEAN.

Scholarly voices across ASEAN have called for effective preparations to cope with environmental change in the region.[9] For example, the Asia-Pacific Centre for Environmental Law (APCEL) at the National University of Singapore convened a conference in 2007, which presented a viable set of proposals for ASEAN-wide action. A planning framework for national strategic action on climate and environmental change has been articulated.[10] Because ASEAN already has cooperative programs on energy and the environment, it could rapidly deploy clean development mechanism (CDM) projects that could further implement sustainable development while averting adverse climate impacts.[11] An

[8] See by analogy the discussion in K. Khoday, "Climate Change as a Threat to Peace and Security: Glacial Melting and Human Security in the Himalayas," in Koh et al., *Crucial Issues in Climate Change and the Kyoto Protocol*. Himalayan glaciers feed the Salween and Mekong river systems in the ASEAN region.

[9] See M. Hossain and E. Selvanathan, *Climate Change and Growth in Asia* (Edward Elgar, 2011).

[10] S. Valentine, "Reframing Global Warming: Toward a Strategic National Planning Framework," in Koh et al., *Crucial Issues in Climate Change and the Kyoto Protocol*, p. 31; K.-L. Koh and L. Bhullar, "Governance on Adaptation to Climate Change in the ASEAN Region," *Carbon and Climate Change Law Review*, 5(1) (2011), pp. 82–90.

[11] J. Lin, "An Overview of the Clean Development Mechanism in Southeast Asia," in Koh et al., *Crucial Issues in Climate Change and the Kyoto Protocol*, p. 99.

ASEAN CDM program could accelerate the installation of energy efficiency and local wind, solar and kinetic energy sources for generating electricity. To cope regionally, and build self-sufficiency, ASEAN member states will need to establish a reliable emissions database, designate the national development authorities to be responsible for ASEAN-wide projects, set up a financing mechanism and auditing procedures, and launch CDM across the region, without waiting for international CDM measures.[12] Since it is likely that not all ASEAN member states are able at once to participate in either a CDM system, or an ASEAN-wide market system for emission trading, ASEAN could launch pilot CDM projects and at the same time build the capacity of all ASEAN member states to join the system.

Reducing Emissions from Deforestation and Forest Degradation (REDD), plus ecosystem conservation (REDD+) is a collaborative program led by the United Nations to address emissions reduction as part of a climate change solution. REDD+ however, includes conservation and sustainable management, and enhancement of forest carbon stock – a mitigation measure closely related to CDM.

[12] International issues that have retarded the value of CDM, under the Kyoto Protocol and otherwise, have been identified, and since these issues remain to be resolved, it is prudent for ASEAN to learn from them and move to develop its own regional base for a CDM program. See C. Streek and J. Lin, "Making Markets Work – A Review of CDM Performance and the Need for Reform," in Koh et al., *Crucial Issues in Climate Change and the Kyoto Protocol*, p. 181; and A. Gunawansa, "The Kyoto Protocol and Beyond: A South Asian Perspective" in ibid., p. 302.

ASEAN has urged developed countries to provide funding on REDD+ to ensure forest dependent livelihoods in ASEAN are sustained.[13]

In November 2012 APCEL organized "Workshop on REDD+ and Legal Regimes of Mangroves, Peatlands and Other Wetlands: ASEAN and the World". The objective of this Workshop was to assist developing countries in ASEAN to put into place legal and policy frameworks and a system for implementation of REDD+ for wetlands. It explored how countries can promote the conservation and management of wetlands through national legislation, and set up the pre-conditions for obtaining greenhouse gas sequestration credits; restore degraded wetlands (particularly peatlands and mangroves) and provide the pre-conditions for potential REDD+ funding; and provide long-term adaptation planning for climate change impacts. While REDD+ is a mitigation strategy, adaptation is necessary for its long-term success as it will depend on the ability of forest and wetland ecosystems to adapt to climate change.

The Workshop also addressed how harmful impacts on wetlands should be considered, in addition to the need for new wetlands to be planted or restored, raising the question

[13] ASEAN Leaders' Statement on Climate Change to the 17th Session of the Conference of the Parties to the United Nations Framework Convention on Climate Change and the 7th Session of the Conference of Parties Serving as the Meeting of Parties to the Kyoto Protocol, Bali, November 17, 2011, www.asean.org/archive/documents/19th%20summit/ASEAN_Leaders'_Statement_on_Climate_Change.pdf.

of the legal process for creating new wetlands, and the need to understand and sustain wetlands in order to preserve human life on Earth in this Anthropocene epoch. The priorities for both future adaptation funding and sequestration funding were discussed, as well as evaluations of gaps in current laws.[14]

Thus, academic and professional prescriptions for how ASEAN can cope with the disruptions of global environmental change are not lacking. What is missing, however, is a scaling up of ASEAN's intergovernmental capacity to accept and act on these recommendations. Southeast Asia is better situated than most regions to act, since it has taken the political decisions to integrate its deliberative and collaborative capacities.

The Fourth ASEAN State of the Environment Report notes that several impacts of climate change will challenge ASEAN member states. All ASEAN member states

[14] A number of papers were presented at the workshop. See, for example, N. A. Robinson, "Mangroves, Peatlands and Other Wetlands: Global Cooperation Among National Programmes," in APCEL and NUS, *Workshop on REDD+ and Legal Regimes of Mangroves, Peatlands and Other Worlds*, Singapore November 15–16, 2012; and K.-L. Koh, "A Survey of ASEAN Instruments Relating to Peatlands, Mangroves and Other Wetlands: the REDD+ Context," ibid., which discusses two instruments on REDD and REDD+, namely, the ASEAN Common Position Paper on Reducing Emissions from Deforestation and Forest Degradation (REDD) in Developing Countries and ASEAN Common Position Paper on Reducing Emission from Deforestation and Forest Degradation Plus (REDD+) in Developing Countries. Other papers included case studies on REDD+ Ready Countries in ASEAN, namely Indonesia, Lao PDR and the Philippines.

have ratified the United Nations Framework Convention on Climate Change[15] and the Kyoto Protocol.[16] ASEAN's Socio-Cultural Council has established the ASEAN Working Group on Climate Change,[17] which has begun consultative and education activities about how to deal with the effects of climate change, as required by the UNFCCC through mitigation of greenhouse gas emissions and through adaptation to the changes induced by climate change. The ASEAN Socio-Community Blueprint[18] focuses on "environmental sustainability"[19] and encourages general approaches to climate change, such as mainstreaming climate change into national development plans, and stakeholder engagement and capacity building. These general themes, however, are essentially an acknowledgment that climate change is a recognized concern, but ASEAN member states have not agreed on more concrete actions. ASEAN does have a "Multi-Sectoral Framework on Climate Change: Agriculture, Fisheries and

[15] United Nations Framework Convention on Climate Change, May 9, 1992, S. Treaty Doc No. 102–38, 1771 U.N.T.S. 107. To date, 195 parties have acceded or ratified the Convention. See UNFCCC, Status of Ratification of the Convention, http://unfccc.int/essential_background/convention/status_of_ratification/items/2631.php.

[16] Kyoto Protocol to The United Nations Framework Convention on Climate Change (Kyoto) UN Doc FCCC/CP/1997/7/Add. 1, December 10, 1997; 37 ILM 22 (1998). To date, 192 parties have acceded or ratified the Protocol. See UNFCCC, Status of Ratification of the Kyoto Protocol, http://unfccc.int/kyoto_protocol/status_of_ratification/items/2613.php.

[17] ASEAN Working Group on Climate Change was established during the 11th ASEAN Ministerial Meeting on the Environment in 2009.

[18] See ASEAN Socio-Community Blueprint.

[19] See ibid., at Section D.

Forestry Toward Food Security,"[20] and has a Strategic Plan of Action on Food Security in the ASEAN Region 2009–2013,[21] but these measures are more a preliminary approach than a coordinated operational system (as, for instance, are the ASEAN natural heritage programs).

In promulgating its food security planning, ASEAN is ahead of many parts of the world. However, as discussed in this chapter, the Fourth ASEAN State of the Environment Report indicates that ASEAN faces many more complex and serious challenges than just the focus on land, forests, water and aquatic resources in relation to food production. Indeed, it has been proposed that the gravity of climate change impacts on the region is such that political security and economic community issues are as essential as socio-cultural issues.[22]

The reality of these climate change-related challenges will become clear as the impacts emerge. Climate change is likely to be the deciding issue that will determine whether ASEAN matures into a forceful regional authority for coordinating how its members will cooperate together for the good of the region and its peoples, or whether it will be only a marginal force. Even where regional cooperation is strong, as in the European Union, there is room

[20] ASEAN Multi-Sectorial Framework on Climate Change and Food Security, endorsed by ASEAN Ministers on Agriculture and Forestry Meeting in 2009.

[21] Strategic Plan of Action on ASEAN Food Security, adopted at the 14th ASEAN Summit in 2009.

[22] Koh and Bhullar, "Governance on Adaptation to Climate Change in the ASEAN Region," p. 82.

for variation in national responses. The Kingdom of the Netherlands, particularly through its Delta Commission's programs,[23] has robust responses under way to cope with the expected adverse effects of climate change. Despite the four Assessment Reports of the Intergovernmental Panel on Climate Change,[24] most regions and nations have yet to act to anticipate and cope with the effects of climate change.

Climate impacts on the ASEAN region are complicated by several factors. Most of the region's population centers and economic activity are located along coastlines, which will be impacted by sea-level rise and coastal surges. Typhoons and other storm patterns concentrate impacts on subregions, and severe weather conditions will impact local areas acutely. As ASEAN's concern for food security indicates, the people of the region depend on production from farming and fishing and natural resources extractions which can be disrupted by climate-related events. The significant levels of poverty across most of the region reduce resilience and exacerbate the adverse impacts of climate disruptions.[25]

Analysis of the five key environmental priority themes identified in Chapter 3 illustrates the gravity of climate impacts in the ASEAN region. No one nation in the

[23] Delta Programme Commissioner, *Delta Programme 2012: Working on the Delta*, www.deltacommissaris.nl/english/Images/11%23094%20Deltaprogramma%202012_EN_def%20internet_tcm310-307583.pdf.

[24] Intergovernmental Panel on Climate Change, Fourth Assessment Reports, www.ipcc.ch/publications_and_data/publications_and_data_reports.shtml#1.

[25] See Koh and Bhullar, "Governance on Adaptation to Climate Change in the ASEAN Region," pp. 83–4.

region can cope with climate change alone. The well-being of the entire region depends on cooperation and collaboration through ASEAN frameworks. Well-being is a core element of the ASEAN Charter, and concerns about how the impacts of climate change can undermine well-being may serve to stimulate ASEAN to develop a regional climate change adaptation program. Non-traditional security concerns may also prompt ASEAN to develop climate change collaborative action plans.

ASEAN can enable the region to pool its knowledge about climate change impacts and trends, and share what it knows. It is not possible for each nation to create its own independent and comprehensive climate programs, because no state has adequate availability of experts, data collection and compilations systems, databases, technologies, or educational or information dissemination processes. ASEAN can provide a real service by assembling the components of a climate change knowledge system and helping to make this system operational. An ASEAN system could then also link to global climate networks, contributing the knowledge of Southeast Asia and benefiting from receiving the knowledge of other regions and of the Earth's systems.

Moreover, the impacts of climate change are so extensive that no nation will have the financial resources alone to cope. Self-reliance systems will need to be developed, such as casualty insurance, and legal and financial frameworks. Existing ASEAN and national systems for disaster relief will need to be complemented by adaptive recovery and building new human settlements in new locations that will enhance their resilience and capability to withstand adverse climate change impacts. Proactive measures to anticipate adverse climate impacts and minimize their damage are needed region-wide, such as planning to retreat from endangered coastal and low-lying settlements and establishing new areas for planting coastal mangroves and wetlands, as well as planting trees in watersheds and on mountainsides. The region's large and small river systems need to learn from the Dutch Delta Commission operations and design appropriate similar modifications to land use in ASEAN member states.

Each of the five key environmental themes that have been evaluated in this monograph, (a) biodiversity and natural and cultural heritage; (b) freshwater resources and forests; (c) marine and coastal resources; (d) human settlements and (e) atmosphere, present issues that ASEAN could be more effectively addressing currently. The climate impacts are happening now, and waiting for future ASEAN studies and consensus before acting will only complicate the magnitude of the problem and difficulties and costs of coping with them. In each of these five areas, the needs of human beings and their dependency on natural systems are given priority, since ASEAN exists for its people. Reliance on the precautionary principle would suggest that ASEAN needs to assist its member states to cut back, suspend or end practices that are demonstrated to exacerbate the negative impacts of climate and other environmental change. Moreover, in order to prepare for the unknown, ASEAN member states will need to implement the resilience principle, and consciously strive to design resilience and redundancy into all human endeavors. Where ASEAN policies and cooperative programs already exist, the door is open to regional action for adapting to the new and coming environmental conditions.

6.1 Flora and fauna and protected areas

ASEAN is among the world's regions with the richest biodiversity. This gives ASEAN an opportunity and better capacity than most regions to sustain ecosystem resilience, and sustain the region's access to ecosystem services and benefits. At the same time, the ASEAN region is losing its biodiversity at a very rapid rate. To stem these losses, regional measures should be given priority: (a) establish marine protected areas over most of the inland waters of the ASEAN region, with limited local uses for sustainable local fishing; (b) establish bio-reserves, along the lines of Brazil, across most of the remaining forested areas and relocate any commercial activity out of those regions and (c) establish a Red List of Endangered Ecosystems and ban harmful activity in those designated ecosystems, and establish in each nation an "ecosystems sustainability service" to monitor and organize law enforcement to ensure protection of the red-listed ecosystems.

The extent to which these recommendations are viewed as extending beyond the existing ASEAN policy and legal frameworks is an indication of the gap that exists between what ASEAN heads of state are currently willing to agree to, and what the scientific, academic and professional experts would advise is needed if ASEAN is to avert a major loss of its ecosystem resilience. The success or failure of ASEAN as a harmonizing force to sustain the region's social and economic and security regimes will depend fundamentally on how it coordinates its environmental systems. The fate of ITL will similarly be determined.

6.2 Fresh water and forests

All river systems, including tributaries and their catchment areas or watersheds, need to be remapped in light of the new flood zone probabilities. Upgradient containments to help reduce flooding and provide for water supplies need to be designed. Small catchment systems are more resilient than large dams, and the "business as usual" approach of large dams needs to be replaced by small area planning and action. Local populations must be mobilized to do much of the work establishing the small catchments and water supply sources.

With rising sea levels, saltwater intrusion along coasts will affect wells near the marine environment, and new systems for potable water need to be prepared. In urban areas, consideration should be given to treating and recycling wastewater and conserving it for human and industrial uses, as is done in London with the Thames and in Singapore.

At the 19th ASEAN Summit held in Bali, on November 17, 2011, the Chairman acknowledged the need for "strong cooperation and coordination among ASEAN member states in enhancing regional capacity on disaster management,"[26] in light of the loss of lives and damage caused by floods from torrential rain that affected countries

[26] Chair's Statement of the 19th ASEAN Summit, Bali, November 17, 2011, www.aseansec.org/documents/19th%20summit/CS.pdf.

in the region. In addition to adopting the ASEAN Leaders' Statement on Cooperation in Flood Prevention, Mitigation, Relief, Recovery and Rehabilitation,[27] the leaders also agreed to strengthen their endeavor in "promoting sustainable usage and management of water resources in the region,"[28] to protect the well-being of all living organisms in ASEAN, including those along the Mekong River and other riverine systems.

International flood control systems are needed for the Mekong and other riverine systems on ASEAN's mainland area. A region-wide programmatic or generic environmental impact assessment is needed for the hydrologic systems, to ensure that all uses of the waters are sustained adaptively, and not sacrificed to designs of the past with large dams.

In 1995, the Governments of Cambodia, Lao PDR, Thailand and Vietnam signed the Agreement on Cooperation for the Sustainable Development of the Mekong River Basin[29] to govern, inter alia, flood control and the environmental integrity of the Mekong River, including maintenance of mainstream flows. The Agreement also established an institutional framework to ensure cooperation in the Mekong River Basin; the Mekong River Commission (MRC) was created for the purposes of the Agreement. In particular, the MRC

[27] ASEAN Leaders' Statement on Cooperation in Flood Prevention, Mitigation, Relief, Recovery and Rehabilitation, Bali, November 17, 2011.

[28] See Chair's Statement of the 19th ASEAN Summit, at p. 17.

[29] Agreement on the Cooperation for the Sustainable Development of the Mekong River Basin, Chiang Rai, Thailand, April 5, 1995, www.kellnielsen.dk/mekong/agreem.htm.

created the Flood Management and Mitigation Program to implement and coordinate flood-management activities such as the issuance of daily flood forecasts and warnings and information exchange with regional and international personnel and organizations.[30] In an effort to further sustainable development in the management of the Mekong Basin, MRC has formed new partnerships and working relationships with several international organizations including ASEAN, the Greater Mekong Sub-region, the Asian Development Bank and the World Bank.

At the First Summit of the Mekong River Commission held in Hua Hin, Thailand, 2010, the Heads of Governments of Cambodia, Lao PDR, Thailand and Vietnam reaffirmed their commitment toward the promotion of "sustainable development, utilization, conservation and management of water and related sources of the Mekong River Basin."[31] Encouraged by the achievements thus far, the parties adopted the MRC Hua Hin Declaration[32] to enhance efforts toward optimization of water resources and mutual benefits for all riparians, and to mitigate adverse effects from natural disasters and/or man-made activities. The Summit was not an ASEAN initiative but that of the MRC (as the Mekong

[30] Flood Management & Mitigation Programme, www.mrcmekong.org/about-the-mrc/programmes/flood-management-and-mitigation-programme/.

[31] MRC Hua Hin Declaration, Meeting the Needs, Keeping the Balance: Towards Sustainable Development of the Mekong River Basin, Hua Hin, April 5, 2010, http://ns1.mrcmekong.org/MRC_news/speeches/MRC-Hua-Hin-Declaration5-Apr-10.htm.

[32] Ibid.

River Basin Agreement, 1995 is not an ASEAN document). However, the four MRC members are also ASEAN member states.

6.3 Marine and coastal resources

The ASEAN coastlines are among the longest in the world, and its archipelagos and bays encompass a vast and bio-rich body of marine living resources. To protect the marine environments, marine protected areas should be established across most of the ASEAN region, and most commercial fishing should be suspended until environmental impact assessments can be made to determine the sustainability of the fisheries. Subsistence local fishing will doubtless continue during such a review, but if the fisheries are not sustained, all local fish resources will be depleted in time.

Each nation should establish systems of adaptive coastal zone management to redesign and relocate land uses on the coasts before they are disrupted by sea-level rise, storm surges and storms. ASEAN should consider establishing an ASEAN-wide coastal zone service to help with the mapping and advising of local authorities.

At the 10th ASEAN Summit held in Vientiane, the Heads of State/Government adopted the Vientiane Action Program (2004–2010) toward realizing the ASEAN Community: the ASEAN Security Community, ASEAN Economic Community and ASEAN Socio-Cultural Community, which promotes environmental sustainability through ecological and natural resource management. In succeeding the Hanoi Plan of Action (1999–2004) that sought, as one of its aims, to protect the marine environment, the Vientiane Action Program "ensure[s] ASEAN's coastal marine environments are sustainably managed, representative ecosystems, pristine areas and species are protected; economic activities are sustainably managed, and public awareness of the coastal and marine environment instilled."[33] Its action plan includes the following key objectives:

> enhance inter-agency and inter-sectoral coordination at the national, regional and international levels for achieving sustainable development of the ASEAN's coastal and marine environment; further expand and implement the ASEAN Marine Water Quality Criteria; and implement the ASEAN Criteria for Marine Heritage Areas, and ASEAN Criteria for National Protected Areas to establish a representative network of protected areas to protect critical habitats.[34]

Prior to the adoption of the Vientiane Action Programme, the ASEAN ministers responsible for the environment had already endorsed the following criteria to ensure joint efforts on a national level to protect the common marine resources in the region: the Marine Water Quality Criteria for the ASEAN Region, the ASEAN Criteria for National Marine Protected Areas and the ASEAN Criteria for Marine Heritage Areas.[35] These criteria set standards to safeguard marine life and human health, as well as benchmarks for designation and supervision of new and existing protected areas.

33 See Vientiane Action Programme, p. 17.

34 Ibid., at p. 43.

35 ASEAN, Press Release, www.aseansec.org/13403.htm.

6.4 Human settlements

6.4.1 Cities

Urban land use and infrastructure policies will need to give priority attention to shifting urban settlements away from identified hazard areas. The implications of a much-altered hydrologic cycle will require redesigning stormwater flows and establishing new water catchment systems and sources of water supplies that can withstand periods of shortage. Moreover, as sea levels rise, urban dwellings will need to be relocated away from the shallow seacoasts.

New housing and physical systems for reducing and recycling solid waste and sanitary waste need to be designed and built rapidly, to provide accommodation for displaced persons. A "design with nature" approach is needed, to provide open space and avoid the "heat island" phenomenon in human settlements. Mass transport systems need to be established, and obsolete transport systems reliant on the internal combustion engine and petrol need to be phased out.

Cities provide the fundamentals for each ASEAN member state's economic, trading, finance and government systems. If the cities fail because they cannot adapt to the new environmental conditions, all economic and governmental activity will decline.

At the 10th ASEAN Ministerial Meeting on Haze held in Siem Reap, Cambodia, (2003) ASEAN Environment Ministers adopted the Regional Environmentally Sustainable Cities Programme (RESCP) and established an ASEAN Working Group on Environmentally Sustainable Cities

(AWGESC) to develop strategies and action plans to drive the implementation of RESCP. Later that year, the AWGESC developed a framework that comprises a comprehensive set of policies, strategies and programs designed to attain environmental sustainability for ASEAN cities under RESCP. The Framework for Environmentally Sustainable Cities in ASEAN was adopted by the ASEAN Environment Ministers at the 9th ASEAN Ministerial Meeting on the Environment. In addition, the AWGESC also proposed an ASEAN Initiative on Environmentally Sustainable Cities, which includes the development of an ASEAN implementation plan for each of twenty-three ASEAN cities and the creation of an ASEAN Network for information exchange and capacity development.[36] Table 6.1 outlines the terms of reference for AWGESC. Integration through law emerges as both a tool and a product of the AWGESC mandate.

At the Third East Asia Summit, sixteen East Asia Summit (EAS) nations signed the Singapore Declaration on Climate Change, Energy and the Environment (2007) in response to the growing concerns about the adverse impacts of climate change on socio-economic development, health and the environment. The EAS includes ASEAN member countries as well as China, Japan, the Republic of Korea, India, Australia and New Zealand. To address environmental challenges posed by growing urbanization in the region, the Declaration seeks to pool together "experiences, expertise

[36] For background information on ASEAN Initiative on Environmentally Sustainable Cities, see http://environment.asean.org/index.php?page=overview:esc:network:background.

Table 6.1 Terms of reference of ASEAN Working Group on Environmentally Sustainable Cities (AWGESC)

Terms of reference
1. To develop a framework for sustainable cities in ASEAN that is applicable to yet accommodate the prevailing but varied circumstances among ASEAN cities.
2. To develop strategies and action plans to realize the vision of sustainable cities in ASEAN.
3. To promote the sharing of information and expertise in environmental protection and management to further enhance environmental sustainability in ASEAN cities.
4. To recommend common targets and indicators to assess sustainability for cities in ASEAN.
5. To facilitate and organise activities, including seminars, workshops, etc. to promote inter-city environmental co-operation and facilitate transfer of know-how and expertise.
6. To foster better understanding and closer co-operation amongst relevant agencies of ASEAN member countries, and international and community-based organizations in the area of urban environmental management and monitoring.
7. To promote public awareness and encourage 3P (Private, Public and People) Sectors' participation in implementing the action programmes to achieve the vision of sustainable cities in ASEAN.

Source: Environmentally Sustainable Cities in ASEAN, www.aseansec.org/awgesc.htm.

and technology in areas such as urban planning including transportation, green buildings, water management, urban greenery and urban biodiversity conservation, sanitation and waste management, 3Rs (Reduce, Reuse and Recycle) and air, noise, water, and land pollution control," and to embrace "initiatives such as 'Low Carbon Society', 'Compact Cities', 'Eco-Cities' and 'Environmentally Sustainable Transport.'"[37]

The EAS nations convened again at the East Asia Summit Conference on Livable Cities in 2008 to discuss, among others, "how East Asian cities could work together to develop sustainable and ecologically friendly cities."[38] Because EAS cities faced common challenges in light of rapid population growth, these cities are committed to addressing these challenges and agreed that the region should work together more actively to promote sustainable and ecologically-friendly communities. In recent years, eco-cities such as the Sino/Singapore Tianjin Eco-city project have been developed in many parts of the world and can be modeled as an adaptation to climate change.[39]

[37] Singapore Declaration on Climate Change, Energy and the Environment, Singapore, November 21, 2007, www.asean.org/21116.htm.

[38] Summary Report of the East Asia Summit Conference on Liveable Cities, Center for Livable Cities, Singapore, June 22–25, 2008, p. 3.

[39] K.-L. Koh, "Eco-Cities as Low Carbon Cities: An Adaptation to Climate Change Node?" in BIT Congress, Inc., *BIT's 1st Annual World Congress of Greentech: Low Carbon Summit*, October 19–21, 2012, Guangdong, China; K.-L. Koh, G. Asanga and L. Bhullar, "'Eco-cities' and 'Sustainable Cities' – Whither?" *Social Space Journal*, Lien Centre for Social Innovation, Singapore Management University, pp. 84–92; The Singapore Declaration on Climate Change, Energy and the Environment, 2007: "Appreciating initiatives such as low carbon society, compact cities, eco-cities and environmentally sustainable transport" in K.-L. Koh, *ASEAN Environmental Law, Policy and Governance*, vol. II (World Scientific, 2009), paragraph 18(b) of Chapter 97.

6.4.2 *Countryside*

"Business as usual" in the development of lands and exploitation of ecosystems is at its end. The Dutch national climate change plan, Delta Commission,[40] has laid out a path forward. Where economic activity must cease or be moved, the government will pay existing land users to leave, and relocation is not optional. Since existing uses will be disrupted in any event, they are compensated for the move but not for what had been the "full market value" since those markets no longer can be predicted to exist. Laws to redefine "property" and "fair compensation" are required, and to provide for Rio Principle 10: giving the public access to participate in the environmental decision-making affecting them, educating them and giving them access to environmental information and access to justice.

It is helpful to recount the experience of Singapore during its period of urban resettlement. In the early years of self-government, Singapore had to clean up rivers and relocate squatter habitations. The government established the Housing and Development Board to provide good and affordable mass-built apartments for the people. Because the Constitution does not provide protection for property, the Land Acquisition Act was enacted to compensate land owners who were dispossessed and squatters who had no title to land. The Act provided compensation at either market value or the value at a particular date, whichever was lower. The issue of "market value" compensation was hotly debated

[40] See Delta Programme Commissioner, *Delta Programme 2012*.

in the Parliament; full market value did not take into account the appreciations in value contributed by the state in providing the infrastructure. It is fitting to note that in 2007, the Act was amended to provide that full market value will be paid in all cases where land is acquired for a public purpose. The Constitution remains unchanged in this respect.

Within ASEAN rural land uses need adjustment. Food supply chains for cities need to be given priority and commercial commodity development phased out until food systems can be stabilized and become resilient. Biological controls for pathogens and zoonotic diseases need to be established and given priority. As discussed earlier in Chapter 5,[41] in an effort to prevent and contain avian influenza so as to reduce risk to human and animal health, ASEAN formulated and adopted no less than ten ASEAN instruments. These instruments aimed at implementing regional activities to prevent transboundary transmission. ASEAN also put in place institutional frameworks and member countries coordinated disease surveillance, effective containment measures, stamping out and vaccination policies, diagnostic capabilities, establishment of disease-free zones, information sharing and emergency preparedness plans.

Because cooperation is needed both at the regional and global level to tackle emerging infectious diseases such as the avian influenza, ASEAN continues to collaborate with ASEAN+3 member countries and international organizations

[41] See also Part V – Health: (Animal and Human) and the Environment – SARS, Avian Influenza and Swine Influenza in Koh, *ASEAN Environmental Law, Policy and Governance*, vol. II, pp. 627–749.

(e.g. the UN, World Health Organization, Food and Agriculture Organization and World Organisation for Animal Health) to increase the effectiveness of disease control. However, there remain areas where ASEAN should consider and collaborate with other organizations calling for integrated approaches toward public health and zoonotic diseases.

Spatial planning for biodiversity corridors and to facilitate resilience in biological systems that sustain ecosystems services needs to be given priority over past practices that degrade and exploit such biological resources. Coastal areas need to be mapped to show where a 3-meter rise in sea level is likely, and the human settlements and uses of these coastlands need to be adjusted and moved inland or to higher elevations. New governmental systems need to be established to provide for adaptive coastal zone management for siting new mangroves, wetlands, ports, kinetic energy sites and other coastal uses.

At the 11th ASEAN Ministerial Meeting on the Environment and the 5th Meeting of the Conference of the Parties to the ASEAN Agreement on Transboundary Haze Pollution, the ASEAN Environment Ministers adopted the Singapore Resolution on Environmental Sustainability and Climate Change.[42] In line with the ASEAN Declaration on Environmental Sustainability signed two years earlier,[43] the resolution embodied future actions in regard to climate

[42] Singapore Resolution on Environmental Sustainability and Climate Change, Singapore, October 29, 2009, www.aseansec.org/documents/Singapore-AMME-Resolution.pdf.

[43] ASEAN Declaration on Environmental Sustainability, Singapore, November 29, 2007, www.aseansec.org/21060.htm.

change, management and protection of the environment, as well as conservation of biodiversity and natural resources in the region. Among others, the ministers called for greater collaboration to achieve the objectives set out in the Convention on Biological Diversity – a multilateral agreement to which all ASEAN member countries have either ratified or acceded to. Notably, the resolution called for increased efforts to reduce forest degradation and deforestation, the creation of alternative livelihood activities and the establishment of more ASEAN Heritage Parks and protected areas.[44] The ministers also urged member countries to support initiatives and programs under the ASEAN Centre for Biodiversity.

6.5 Atmosphere

The burning of forests, wetlands, mangroves and peatlands needs to be stopped at once, and measures to restore the depleted resources begun. The sources of the "Haze" are not sustainable. More biomass needs to be planted to restore lost photosynthesis capacity in the region.[45]

It is likely that atmospheric brown cloud will persist for some years, until China abates its urban and industrial air pollution. The atmospheric brown cloud actually helps reduce atmospheric temperatures in the region by reflecting solar radiation back into space, but as China cleans up its air pollution, this inadvertent benefit will be lost and temperatures

[44] See Singapore Resolution on Environmental Sustainability and Climate Change.

[45] See APCEL and NUS, *Workshop on REDD+*.

will increase in the ASEAN region. To prepare for this likelihood, building designs to vent heated air and urban design to plant trees and promote cooling conditions will be needed across the entire ASEAN region. It seems unlikely that an atmospheric brown cloud treaty, like the Geneva Convention on Long-distance Air Pollution, will be sought in the ASEAN area, since it would have to involve major industrial powers such as China and Japan with interests different from those of ASEAN states, so the local approach to the heating of the air is a higher priority for ASEAN member states.

Recognizing the vulnerability of the region to the effects of climate change, the Heads of State/Government adopted the ASEAN Leaders' Statement on Climate Change at the 17th Session of the Conference of the Parties to the United Nations Framework Convention on Climate Change (UNFCCC) and the 7th Session of the Conference of Parties Serving as the Meeting of Parties to the Kyoto Protocol at the 19th ASEAN Summit.[46] The Statement urged parties to work together toward reducing greenhouse gas emissions to "hold the increase in global average temperature below 2°C above pre-industrial levels"[47] and to "engage in scientific and technical cooperative activities among ASEAN countries."[48]

[46] ASEAN Leaders' Statement on Climate Change to the 17th Session of the Conference of the Parties to the United Nations Framework Convention on Climate Change and the 7th Session of the Conference of Parties Serving as the Meeting of Parties to the Kyoto Protocol, Bali, November 17, 2011, www.asean.org/archive/documents/19th%20summit/ASEAN_Leaders'_Statement_on_Climate_Change.pdf.

[47] Ibid., p. 3.

[48] Ibid.

The Chair's Statement of the 19th ASEAN Summit reaffirmed ASEAN's strong commitment to develop a platform and action plans to address climate change "both in mitigation and adaptation at the global level to ensure fair, effective and equitable outcome for a new climate change regime."[49] The Summit, themed "ASEAN Community in a Global Community of Nations," was convened to solicit cooperation in the region to reach the ASEAN Community by 2015. On November 22, 2015, the Kuala Lumpur Declaration on the Establishment of the ASEAN Community by December 31, 2015, was formerly declared.[50] As the discussion of these five themes indicates, much remains to be accomplished if the ASEAN member states are to be ready to cope with the effects of climate change. Measured by the incremental accomplishments and evolving consensus, ASEAN's environmental cooperation is exemplary. Climate change will call on ASEAN and each of its member states to undertake pervasive adaptations in order to safeguard past investments for sustainable development. ASEAN has made significant progress in establishing legal frameworks for environmental protection, but this progress has come too late to have had a measurable impact on reversing the regions' trends that show degradation in environmental quality and natural resources. Despite their environmental laws, ASEAN member states still treat the environment as

[49] See Chair's Statement of the 19th ASEAN Summit, p. 22.

[50] www.asean.org/images/2015/November/KL-Declaration/KL%20Declaration%20on%20Establishment%20of%20ASEAN%20Community%202015.pdf.

a cornucopia to be exploited for all it can provide to meet short-term economic objectives. In fact, even without considering climate change, natural products from the region are either in decline or already lost. The gross national product measures only harvests and commodities produced, and do not measure the loss of natural capital. The accounts of natural capital, when consulted, demonstrate that the past or current levels of gross national product among ASEAN member states cannot be sustained.

Climate change is impacting the region, as it is all regions, in irreversible ways. ASEAN cannot sustain its political, legal and social accomplishments, unless it adapts them to climate change. It has perhaps a decade to do so, before the disruptive events of climate change render it so very difficult to do so that it may appear no longer possible.

Chapter 7

Conclusions: ASEAN's challenging way forward

In a region as vast and diverse as ASEAN is in its political, legal, cultural and social systems, it is not surprising that national interests often take precedence over regional interests. It must be recognized that national priorities for the alleviation of poverty in member states take precedence over what many still perceive to be lofty ideals of environmental sustainability. Most political and economic leaders do not yet accept "sustainable development," however short-sighted that may be. Many new and emerging environmental problems have left policy makers in ASEAN, like the rest of the world, wrestling with how best to tackle these issues. These uncertainties are compounded by other factors that come into play, such as the repeated financial crises that may prevent environment-related decisions from moving forward. It also takes time to change deep-seated mindsets of policy makers and other stakeholders in regard to environmental issues.

While ASEAN has progressed at a pace that is comfortable for all states in the region, in an organic, evolutionary way, the environment lacks such luxury of time. Environmental disruption is growing across ASEAN, and climate change and other environmental disasters call into question the gradualist approach that has characterized ASEAN's past patterns of integration through law.

A more integrated, cohesive ASEAN can emerge from ASEAN's people-to-people approach of those who "think ASEAN." This evolved ASEAN Way would reflect consensus in favor of rapid development of action plans and collaboration. It would recognize that the region has a need to care for ASEAN as an integrated community, with shared values and a common vision.

At present this vision is not a reality, but a long-term goal, and ASEAN continues to reiterate the importance of environmental cooperation (as in other areas) to achieve its vision as it does in the Bangkok Resolution on ASEAN Environmental Cooperation 2012. While it has not been achieved much hope lies in ASEAN young people. ASEAN is actively engaging youth in the region to promote ASEAN identity through cultural heritage and other methods such as environmental education to impart knowledge and awareness. To that end, ASEAN has adopted an ASEAN Environmental Education Action Plan. For ASEAN to realize its vision, there must be a change of mindset that no longer considers integration as interference in internal affairs, in the traditional sense. A distinction ought to be drawn between the principle of "non-interference" in a state's internal affairs and the principle of mutual aid with legitimate assistance or enhanced cooperation in light of environmental disasters.

ASEAN has encountered obstacles in its progress toward integration, especially where there is politicization of issues and where geo-political international relations stand in the way of action on shared environmental principles. Indeed, this monograph's brief survey of ASEAN's evolution has revealed a myriad of challenges facing ASEAN today.

There are two priority areas for ASEAN, namely, development of a more cohesive ASEAN community internally and defining an ASEAN identity to strengthen integration between ASEAN and the global community externally. This approach is realized through programs designed to narrow the development divide and provide a framework for regional cooperation through the Initiative of ASEAN Integration Strategic Framework and Work Plan II (2009–2015).

At the 45th ASEAN Ministerial Meeting held in Cambodia in July 2012, the summit broke up without issuing a joint communique on the concerns of ASEAN over worsening maritime disputes between China and several ASEAN member states[1] in the South China Sea. For the first time in the forty-five years of the Association's history, there was a public failure in demonstrating solidarity and cohesiveness. Critics have pointed out that even when the ASEAN Way has fallen by the wayside in the past, it had always managed to find compromise solutions to disputes. In the South China Sea dispute, solutions are ongoing.

In spite of the political nature of the maritime dispute of an area rich in natural resources such as oil, minerals and fish, there are also environmental implications. What has emerged thus far in this dispute is a big-power rivalry between China and the United States; the latter aimed at undercutting China's influence throughout the region. This poses great challenges for ASEAN as it seeks to maintain its

[1] The ASEAN member states involved in the dispute are: Cambodia, Vietnam, Philippines and Malaysia.

central role in furtherance of its interests and to foster cohesiveness, previously discussed in Chapter 5.

Moreover, ASEAN has to further instill upon member states and its peoples that they have to work toward a destiny that requires a "new thinking" envisaged by the late S. Rajaratnam, First Foreign Affairs Minister of Singapore, at the opening ceremony of the inaugural meeting of ASEAN Foreign Ministers in 1967:

> It is easy to give birth to a new organization … Now the really difficult task is to give flesh and blood to this concept … The realization has grown and, therefore, it is necessary for us if we are really to be successful in giving life to ASEAN to marry national thinking with regional thinking. We must now think at two levels. We must think not only of our national interests but posit them against regional interests. That is a new way of thinking of our problems. And that is two different things and sometimes they can conflict. Secondly, we must also accept the fact, if we are really serious about it, that regional existence means painful adjustments to those practices and thinking in our respective countries. If we are not going to do that, then regionalism remains Utopia.[2]

Forty-eight years later, has a "new way of thinking" permeated the efforts of ASEAN in developing environmental sustainability? Many have criticized the ASEAN Way as one of the stumbling blocks in institutional building and integration

[2] Statement of H. E. S. Rajaratnam, Minister of Foreign Affairs, Singapore, at the Opening Ceremony of the Inaugural Meeting of Foreign Ministers of ASEAN, Bangkok, August 8, 1967.

of environmental law. While the Association has correspondingly calibrated the ASEAN Way to rectify principles of sovereignty and non-intervention, the fact remains that these principles are now embedded in the ASEAN Charter. Thus, the challenge lies in giving a robust interpretation of the securitization of transnational and/or transboundary environmental challenges, particularly in new and emerging environmental issues under the ASEAN Political-Security Community (APSC) Blueprint. How the new approach will play out remains to be tested, but recent events that prompt collaboration, such as responses to Cyclone Nargis, or the flooding in Thailand and Typhoon Bopha in the Philippines, give a glimmer of hope.

There is a need to bridge the gap between public law and relations, and environmental law. Transboundary environmental challenges under APSC have opened the door to new and emerging environmental issues to be framed on an "ASEAN-centric," "member state-centric" and human-centric approach. The "three-in-one" approach however, poses a great challenge to ASEAN because it appears to be contradictory under the traditional approach and contrary to international law, though the discourse has yet to be developed. ASEAN is at a crossroad, and so is the world. An integrated approach involves extension of the environmental discourse into relevant sectors so as to make them holistic. It is especially significant at this time because ASEAN and the international community are experiencing unprecedented environmental challenges that require enhanced coordination and cooperation at a global level. The writers wonder if perhaps the UN initiative on Responsibility to Protect[3] can be adopted to strengthen the non-traditional security approach.

As discussed previously in this study, ASEAN is focused on narrowing the development gap between Cambodia, Lao PDR, Myanmar and Vietnam states and the rest of the region as a precondition to alleviating poverty and achieving regional integration. In doing so, it serves to promote ASEAN's centrality in the broader regional affairs so as to play a more active role in global governance. At the 20th ASEAN Summit, the Chair "underlined that regional and global challenges go beyond national boundaries and would require a more cooperative and comprehensive approach, particularly through regional integration." The Initiative of ASEAN Integration Work Plan (2009–2015) has made progress in regional integration, as well as narrowing the development gap in an ASEAN community-building process, but much more work needs to be done.

After the 2012 UN Rio+20 Conference, it was noted that "National Legislatures, environmental ministries and courts have implemented and applied congruent programs for environmental sustainability world-wide."[4] The Principles of the UN Rio Declaration on Environment and Development have been incorporated into national constitutions and laws, including ASEAN states. The Rio+20 outcome document,

[3] International Coalition for the Responsibility to Protect, An Introduction to the Responsibility to Protect, www.responsibilitytoprotect.org/index.php/about-rtop/learn-about-rtop.

[4] N. A. Robinson, "Reflecting on Measured Deliberations," 42 *Envtl. L. & Pol'y* 219 (2012), http://digitalcommons.pace.edu/cgi/viewcontent.cgi?article=1846&context=lawfaculty.

entitled "The Future We Want," called for more effective intergovernmental cooperation such as in the area of adaptation to climate change, which is a global priority. As a regional organization, ASEAN already promotes the implementation of Agenda 21, Rio+20 and Multilateral Environmental Agreements. Much remains to be done, but the process is under way.

An illustration of ASEAN's capacity for integration through law is found in ASEAN's recent efforts in response to water-related disaster management, pursuant to the ASEAN Agreement on Disaster Management and Emergency Response. ASEAN successfully put into action objectives of the Agreement through the AADMER Work Programme (2010–2015) and the establishment of the ASEAN-Emergency Rapid Assessment Team. To further illustrate its key role, ASEAN has entered into a Tripartite Memorandum of Cooperation with the UN International Strategy for Disaster Risk Reduction and the World Bank on Disaster Reduction in the Region. ASEAN has also joined efforts with the UN for the coordination of disasters[5] and has established the ASEAN Humanitarian Assistance Center to strengthen disaster management strategies. The lessons learned from Typhoon Yolanda has further strengthened ASEAN's resolve to manage future disasters more effectively.

At this juncture, it is pertinent to refer to the Mid-Term Review of the ASEAN Socio-Cultural Community (ASCC)

[5] Joint Declaration on ASEAN-UN Collaboration in Disaster Management, Ha Noi, October 30, 2010, www.asean.org/asean/asean-summit/item/joint-declaration-on-asean-un-collaboration-in-disaster-management.

Blueprint (2009–2015) Executive Summary: Adopted by the ASEAN Leaders at the 23rd ASEAN Summit.[6] As stated in its Executive Summary, the purpose of the Mid-Term Review, inter alia, is to assess (i) whether the measures and actions of the ASCC have been effectively implemented at the national and regional levels; (ii) whether it has achieved the goals of the ASCC; (iii) means of implementation; (iv) institutional mechanisms and (v) availability of financial resources to sustain the achievement by the end of 2015. It also contains a recommendation to enhance the timely and effective implementation of ASCC by the end of 2015.

The time frame for assesssment of effective implementation in the Mid-Term Review is the end of December 2015 – the date of the coming into effect of the ASEAN Community. The Mid-Term Review assessment criteria of ASCC are relevance, effectiveness, efficiency, sustainability and impact. The question of the extent cooperation and integration is needed at the vertical integration (national and ASEAN, and ASEAN and the global community); or horizontal (across ASEAN countries) was not really addressed. However, in "Ways Forward, Beyond 2015" the phrase "a more *integrated* ASEAN Economic Community" (emphasis added) is mentioned in the context of a need for ASCC to position itself to sustain an environment in the midst of a more integrated ASEAN Economic Community, along with a more peaceful and stable APSC. A "people-centered" approach is also important – this suggests that the forging of

[6] The ASEAN Secretariat, Jakarta, 2014, www.asean.org/images/resources/2014/Apr/FA_Executive_Summary_FINAL-WEB[1].pdf.

an ASEAN identity discussed in our analysis (an impossible dream, at the moment) needs to have a common value system to facilitate integration.[7] But this is only one mechanism and other factors have to be considered.

Our analysis shows that implementation depends more on cooperation (which is not integration but may result in integration) rather than integration, for a variety of reasons. The Bangkok Resolution on ASEAN Environmental Cooperation 2012 calls for further cooperation to strengthen regional commitments and to realize the implementation of ASCC to achieving the ASEAN Vision of a "Clean and Green ASEAN," the protection of the environment, the sustainability of natural resources and the high quality of life of its peoples. It also calls on its member countries to promote the mainstreaming of sustainable development at all levels and "integrate sustainable consumption and production (SCP) patterns into our national policies which is fundamental in addressing all aspects of environmental sustainability." As this is within the national level context, no obstacles of sovereignty and non-intervention arise – integration at national level is possible. This could be with "mainstreaming." United Nations Post-2015 Sustainable Development Goals, which call for the action-oriented achievement of sustainable development by 2030 will give impetus to ASEAN to meet this goal.[8]

[7] K.-L. Koh, "ASEAN Cultural Heritage – Forging an Identity for Realisation of an ASEAN Community in 2015," in *Third International Symposium of Laureates Elizabeth Haub Prizes for Environmental Law Diplomacy, Environmental Policy & Law* (IOS Press 2014), p. 237.

[8] www.google.com.sg/?gfe_rd=cr&ei=MR5wU5jXBoSQiAfMoYGABw#q=un+sustainable+development+goals+pdf.

With increased frequency of climate change-related activities in ASEAN and around the world, whether natural or human-induced, a global approach toward cooperation has emerged in response to disaster management. The challenge lies in how this will work out effectively in the future. ASEAN is at the crossroads between sustaining economic prosperity and tackling climate change, with its threats of environmental disasters in the near term. In fact, one of the greatest challenges is to build a disaster-resilient ASEAN. As ASEAN looks forward in its cooperation for the twenty-first century, there are several key issues that deserve focus.

First, "chronic crisis" management: ASEAN has been collaborating on disaster relief, but this emergency response issue is very different than tackling chronic crises. For example, sea levels will rise 1 to 3 meters across the ASEAN region in the next 50 to 100 years, or less. There is an urgent need to prepare for a systematic retreat from the seacoasts. This requires a phased redevelopment. Regions that are at risk must be identified and inland regions prepared with ample water and sewage treatment facilities, housing and education facilities, as well as new jobs, to relocate the coastal communities. Raising funds by floating public bonds is difficult because of the way in which such debt refinancing has played since the recession of 2008. Such bonds are usually issued for thirty to forty years. Thus, to use public financing, the society needs to think forty years ahead. We must plan our land use redesign and resettlement systems to provide new communities such as, if necessary, for climatic migrants, and these places need to be ready in twenty years. The "rebirth" of the Singapore River demonstrates that where there is political will, it can be done.[9] True, this is in a different context. But it is an inspiration for ASEAN to develop its planning systems in its agenda now, if it is to happen efficiently and with economic and ecological sustainability inside each ASEAN member state.

Second, each ASEAN member state should reach into its cultural roots and reveal the social and ecological principles of sustainability within each of the respective national cultures. These ecological and cultural community relationships and their norms have more in common than the respective economic levels of economic development in each nation. Norms of ecological and community sustainability must reassert themselves for environmental sustainability to take root. Resilience and self-sufficiency are the foundations of any regional or global trading system; if nations loose these roots, then regional or global free trade weakens their national capacity for sustainability and trade erodes further. So, ASEAN member states should first reaffirm their national Agenda 21 foundations, then look to their regional ASEAN partnerships, and then look to wider economic relationships, and not the other way around. These consensual and regional relationships have the authenticity and are rooted in culture and are the cultural and moral foundations for the ASEAN Way.

Third, the challenge for ASEAN, as for all nations and the UN system as a whole, is to cope with the conditions of life in the Anthropocene. Most nations prefer the

[9] www.singapore-river.com/history-singapore-river; www.rhuf.net/ita/download/Singapore%20River.pdf.

"old shoe" of business as usual in the Holocene epoch. As Nobel Laureate Paul Crutzen and others explain in the journal *Ambio*, business as usual cannot sustain contemporary human socio-economic life into the future.[10] ASEAN has not reflected upon the transformative environmental changes of the coming decades. ASEAN's greatest challenges lie ahead. These will test whether integration through law can be realized.

Though ASEAN has formulated a non-traditional approach, previously discussed in Chapter 5, to effectively deal with transnational and/or transboundary environmental issues, it has on several occasions taken a step back for fear that the new approach may erode principles of sovereignty and non-intervention. Following the United Nations Security Council debate on the security implications of climate change and their impacts on conflict issues such as energy, water, food and displacement of populations, the former Secretary-General of ASEAN, Surin Pitsuwan called for a similar approach. He points out that human security needs a new mindset and requires a new look at the issue of security, because certain transboundary environmental issues will impact on human security.[11]

Fourth, non-governmental organizations and civil society organizations should be given greater participation

[10] W. Steffen, P. J. Crutzen, J. R. McNeill, "The Anthropocene: Are Humans Now Overwhelming the Great Forces of Nature?" *Ambio*, 36(8) (December 2007), p. 614.

[11] S. Pitsuwan, Keynote Address, "Launch of the RSIS Centre for Non-Traditional Security Studies," Singapore, May 6, 2008.

rights in the ASEAN processes. The ASEAN Law Association can also play a greater role in legal integration efforts within ASEAN. In the words of former Secretary-General of the United Nations, Kofi Annan, "Our biggest challenge in this new century is to take an idea that seems abstract – sustainable development – and turn it into all the world's people." The "world's people" should include the voices of those who should have a say in turning the abstract of sustainable development into reality, and these voices are crucial if the ASEAN community is to be inclusive pursuant to the ASEAN Charter and ASCC.[12]

Fifth, it must be emphasized that effective governance and management of the environment should begin at the national level. Because implementation of international and multinational environmental agreements is dependent on an effective national environmental law regime, member states should critically examine their laws and institutions to address inadequacies. The region should also seek to harmonize environmental quality standards – a call made back in 1994 in the Bandar Seri Begawan Resolution on Environmental and Development.[13] Laws are only part of the

[12] See, for example, "ASEAN People's Assembly Calls for Greater Participation as ASEAN Turns 40," www.aseanhrmech.org/news/asean-peoples-assembly-greater-participation.html.

[13] See Bandar Seri Begawan Resolution on Environment and Development, Bandar Seri Begawan, April 26, 1994, reproduced in ASEAN Strategic Plan of Action (including Ministerial Resolutions), ASEAN Secretariat, Jakarta, 1994, at 63–5, and reproduced in K.-L. Koh, *ASEAN Environmental Law, Policy and Governance*, (World Scientific, 2009) 78–9; discussed in N. A. Robinson, "Strengthening Sustainable Development in Regional Inter-Governmental

formula for sound environmental management, so they must be supported by institutional, administrative and infrastructural capacity.

Accordingly member states must develop internal capacity, though more robust assistance could be provided to developing states through the implementation of regional and national partnerships. It has been proposed that member states that are more developed could strengthen their efforts to assist developing states in capacity-building programs in environmental law, governance and management. Capacity-building initiatives led by the International Union for the Conservation of Nature Commission on Environmental Law and Asia-Pacific Centre for Environmental Law in 1997 and 1998 ought to be revived and reinvigorated, for these initiatives conducted intensive training programs on environmental law for law professors in the Asia-Pacific Region. Training programs led by institutions in member states could be strengthened with additional monetary funding, or with increased joint participation with other relevant institutions in the region.[14]

Integration through environmental law is a work in progress in ASEAN. This study has elucidated the practice and promise of ASEAN's environmental systems. The journalist Kavi Chongkittavon has written, in

Governance: Lessons from the 'ASEAN Way,'" *Pace Law Faculty Publication*, Paper 371 (2002), pp. 640–82.

[14] This fits into the ASEAN Plan on Environmental Education. See the ASEAN Environmental Education Action Plan Philippine Initiatives 2009–2011, www.emb.gov.ph/eeid/2011/ASEAN/aseanee2011.pdf.

"ASEAN in Transition: Challenges for Viet Envoy as New Secretary-General"[15] that ASEAN urgently needs to build deeper and sustainable common ground. Whatever the new ASEAN Secretary-General "does and says will have an impact on ASEAN integration and identity." This reality underlines the importance of ASEAN integration and identity in all contexts including environment.

From the viewpoint of developing ASEAN integration through environmental law, the two basic assumptions of ASEAN that have influenced ASEAN's role in developing environmental sustainability need to be re-examined. These assumptions are: first, ASEAN should be allowed to continue to develop in a gradual and evolutionary way, at a pace comfortable to all member states. Second, the ASEAN Way (sovereignty and non-interference in the affairs of one another), of decision-making is the bedrock of regional order. Events, particularly the impacts of climate change, will cause ASEAN to explore a more ambitious environmental vision, a calibrated approach to bring about a more robust approach in dealing with vulnerabilities and in building resilience. This coming exploration will transform ASEAN Itself.

ASEAN is not an "island" but is interconnected with the Earth and its world of all nations and all environmental problems. The vulnerabilities that ASEAN and its peoples face will come to take precedence over any obstacles that appear to stand in the way of a "whole-of-ASEAN approach."

[15] *The Straits Times*, January 2, 2013. The Vietnamese diplomat, Le Luong Minh succeeded Surin Pitsuwan on January 1, 2013; the term is for five years.

The vision of ASEAN integrated with the world was demonstrated by ASEAN's successful collaboration in handling Cyclone Nargis and typhoon Haiyan/Yolanda. ASEAN has many examples of successful integration through law, and its member states can nourish these patterns. ASEAN cooperation for sustainability is transcending ASEAN's earlier beliefs in "non-interference" and builds foundations for peace and sustainable development.

One final word. While the focus of this monograph is "integration through law" in the environmental context, it is part of a larger project of integration in the political security, economic and socio-cultural pillars of ASEAN. Hence, integration in environmental law must also be part of the vision to bring about an ASEAN community as envisaged in the ASEAN Charter.[16]

[16] Under the 2015 Kuala Lumpur Declaration on the Establishment of the ASEAN Community, the ASEAN Community was formally established on December 31, 2015. The Declaration aims to establish a "truly rules-based, people-oriented, people-centered ASEAN Community where our peoples continue to participate in and benefit fully from the on-going process of ASEAN integration and community building": www.miti.gov.my/miti/resources/2015_Kuala_Lumpur_Declaration_on_the_Establishment_of_the_ASEAN_Community.pdf. See also *ASEAN 2025: Forging Ahead Together*: www.britcham.org.sg/files/images/pdfs/ASEAN-2025-Forging-Ahead-Together.pdf.

EXECUTIVE SUMMARY

The word "integration" means different things in different contexts. As this monograph is part of a series entitled Integration through Law: The Role of Law and the Rule of Law in ASEAN Integration (ITL) (see General Editors' Preface), it examines the extent ASEAN environmental law contributes to ASEAN regional integration as an ASEAN community. ASEAN's historic transition, from an association in 1967 to its development into a community by December 31, 2015, has seen an evolution in various sectors, not least in environment.

The Introduction to the volume sets the scene, providing an overview of ASEAN and its efforts at regionalism. The history of colonization is noted, which explains the strong emphasis on Westphalian concepts of sovereignty and non-interference with domestic affairs. The efforts at regional integration in the context of the environment closely follow the global environmental movement, from the Stockholm Conference in 1972, to the Rio Conference in 1992 and Agenda 21, which prompted ASEAN's Strategic Plan of Action on the Environment and other initiatives. The ASEAN Way, which involves consensus, respect for the principle of sovereignty and non-intervention, and its challenges and evolution in the context of rapid economic and climatic changes and their deleterious impacts on the environment, are the subject of the chapters that follow.

Chapter 1, ASEAN and environmental sustainability, elaborates on the ASEAN vision of "One Caring and Sharing Community," aspiring toward sustainable development as a common, uniting goal. It examines the difficulties of achieving the five-year plans of action, making the point that the ASEAN Way "makes for informality, quiet diplomacy, face saving and avoidance of legal instruments i.e. hard law." However, some successes in hard law are mentioned, particularly the coming into effect of the ASEAN Transboundary Haze Agreement, with ratification by Indonesia, the last state to do so.

Chapter 2, Integrating sustainability into ASEAN state practice, discusses the importance of environmental governance and environmental management systems. The study finds that national environmental law regimes and governance are uneven across the ASEAN member states, and considerable capacity building is required. The issue of "integration through law" is examined from two perspectives – institutional integration and integration of laws and policies. It lauds the success in the stewardship of the region's terrestrial biological resources while noting the lack of concerted policies to safeguard marine natural resources.

Chapter 3, The environment in the ASEAN region, examines the state of the environment in the ASEAN region in the context of five key issues: biological and natural heritage; fresh water and forests; marine and coastal resources; human settlements; and the atmosphere. These issues are discussed in the context of national laws and the mounting challenges in the region, particularly the increasing loss of biological resources and the adverse impacts of climate change. This study notes that the disruptions resulting from environmental degradation exacerbated by the effects of climate change will undermine efforts at legal integration in ASEAN.

Chapter 4 focuses on the environmental sustainability laws of each ASEAN member state. It briefly discusses each state's legal system and examines its constitution for provisions on protection of the environment. It discusses regional and international efforts at collaboration on environmental issues and laws and, again, examines these issues in the context of the five key issues. There is considerable progress in the protection of biodiversity, natural and cultural heritage (e.g. the ASEAN Declaration on Heritage Parks and the setting up of the ASEAN Centre for Biodiversity) as well as in the tackling of wildlife trade (the establishment of the ASEAN Wildlife Enforcement Network). It notes that while ASEAN member states have enacted a considerable body of environmental legislation, these laws are not yet aligned to work in tandem to advance the policies and programs of ASEAN. There is a need for ASEAN to prioritize education, training and resource allocation. More needs to be done to advance integration through environmental laws.

A number of typologies – from harmonization of environmental sustainability policies, standard setting and hard laws (e.g. the ASEAN Agreement on Transboundary Pollution, 2005), to ASEAN's role in facilitating the implementation of multilateral environmental agreements by its member states – are captured in Chapter 5, ASEAN collaboration toward environmental sustainability, which traces its cooperation before and after the ASEAN Charter 2007. Six case studies including avian influenza, "haze" and wildlife crimes illustrate a mixed report of success, or less than satisfactory implementation. The obstacles that account for ineffective implementation are narrated in this chapter.

Climate disruption and ASEAN's response merited a separate Chapter 6. Such disruption will complicate ASEAN's efforts to build sustainable development across all member states. The impacts will either be a force for strengthening environmental safeguards needed to cope with climate change and thus enhance legal integration or the disruptions will have a disintegration effect. The dynamics affecting decisions about integration through law in the context of responding to climate change depend on how climate change will affect the natural biological resources of Southeast Asia. How each ASEAN member state responds to these challenges will measure the success or failure of its socio-economic development.

Given the diversity in its political, legal, cultural and social systems and the fact that it is not a homogenous group but one that had encountered and is still encountering hostility or disagreement on some issues, tensions between national interests and that of the region are not surprising. While there is no war, and this speaks well for ASEAN, resistance to cooperation has manifested itself in the unjustifiable application of the principles of sovereignty and non-interference in domestic affairs. These principles are embodied in the ASEAN Charter, even though it, together with the ASEAN Roadmap and other instruments aim to integrate environmental policies intra-ASEAN and also with the global community, as demonstrated in several chapters. Other than political obstacles, the challenges posed by the nature of environmental issues –*sans frontières*, interdisciplinary and much else, and without an effective governance system to connect them – have often rendered ineffective the many laws in its member states. This is discussed in Chapter 4, where a review of each member state's environmental legislation illustrates that ASEAN displays both centrifugal and disparate tendencies in legal integration. ASEAN cooperation seeks harmonization and integration to facilitate steps toward region-wide environmental sustainability.

Chapter 7 concludes by reflecting on the challenges and highlighting several key areas for special focus. While concluding that integration through environmental law remains an ongoing "work in progress," it is remarkable how considerable the progress has been since 1967. The monograph ends on a positive note, because ASEAN cooperation for sustainability is clearly transcending ASEAN's early insistence on "non-interference" and is evolving into "enhanced cooperation." This is a positive way of viewing cooperation rather than the negative posture that it is interference. In adopting this stance, ASEAN builds foundations for peace and development.

Appendix A

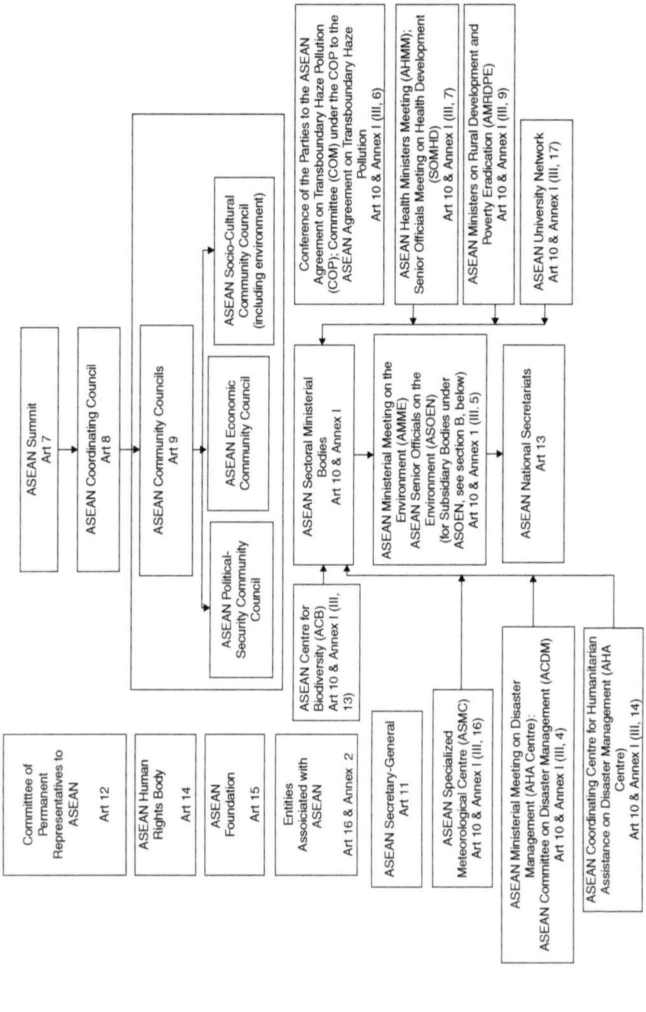

ASEAN organizational structure relevant to the environment – the ASEAN Charter

Appendix B

Founding of ASEAN – a short history

From the ASEAN web page: www.asean.org/asean/about-asean/history

On August 8, 1967, five leaders – the Foreign Ministers of Indonesia, Malaysia, the Philippines, Singapore and Thailand – sat down together in the main hall of the Department of Foreign Affairs building in Bangkok, Thailand and signed a document. By virtue of that document, the Association of Southeast Asian Nations (ASEAN) was born. The five Foreign Ministers who signed it – Adam Malik of Indonesia, Narciso R. Ramos of the Philippines, Tun Abdul Razak of Malaysia, S. Rajaratnam of Singapore and Thanat Khoman of Thailand – would subsequently be hailed as the Founding Fathers of probably the most successful intergovernmental organization in the developing world today. And the document that they signed would be known as the ASEAN Declaration.

It was a short, simply-worded document containing just five articles. It declared the establishment of an Association for Regional Cooperation among the Countries of Southeast Asia to be known as the Association of Southeast Asian Nations (ASEAN) and spelled out the aims and purposes of that Association. These aims and purposes were about cooperation in the economic, social, cultural, technical, educational and other fields, and in the promotion of regional peace and stability through abiding respect for justice and the rule of law and adherence to the principles of the United Nations Charter. It stipulated that the Association would be open for participation by all States in the Southeast Asian region subscribing to its aims, principles and purposes. It proclaimed ASEAN as representing "the collective will of the nations of Southeast Asia to bind themselves together in friendship and cooperation and, through joint efforts and sacrifices, secure for their peoples and for posterity the blessings of peace, freedom and prosperity."

It was while Thailand was brokering reconciliation among Indonesia, the Philippines and Malaysia over certain disputes that it dawned on the four countries that the moment for regional cooperation had come or the future of the region would remain uncertain. Recalls one of the two surviving protagonists of that historic process, Thanat Khoman of Thailand: "At the banquet marking the reconciliation between the three disputants, I broached the idea of forming another organization for regional cooperation with Adam Malik. Malik agreed without hesitation but asked for time to talk with his government and also to normalize relations with Malaysia now that the confrontation was over. Meanwhile, the Thai Foreign Office prepared a draft charter of the new institution. Within a few months, everything was ready. I therefore invited the two former members of the Association for Southeast Asia (ASA), Malaysia and the Philippines, and Indonesia, a key member, to a meeting in Bangkok. In addition, Singapore sent S. Rajaratnam, then Foreign Minister, to see me about joining the new set-up. Although the new organization was planned to comprise only the ASA members plus Indonesia, Singapore's request was favorably considered."

And so in early August 1967, the five Foreign Ministers spent four days in the relative isolation of a beach resort in Bang Saen, a coastal town less than a hundred kilometers southeast of Bangkok. There they negotiated over that document in a decidedly informal manner which they would later delight in describing as "sports-shirt diplomacy." Yet it was by no means an easy process: each man brought into the deliberations a historical and political perspective that had no resemblance to that of any of the others. But with goodwill and good humor, as often as they huddled at the negotiating table, they finessed their way through their differences as they lined up their shots on the golf course and traded wisecracks on one another's game, a style of deliberation which would eventually become the ASEAN ministerial tradition.

Now, with the rigors of negotiations and the informalities of Bang Saen behind them, with their signatures neatly attached to the ASEAN Declaration, also known as the Bangkok Declaration, it was time for some formalities. The first to speak was the Philippine Secretary of Foreign Affairs, Narciso Ramos, a one-time journalist and long-time legislator who had given up a chance to be Speaker of the Philippine Congress to serve as one of his country's first diplomats. He was then sixty-six years old and his only son, the future President Fidel V. Ramos, was serving with the Philippine Civic Action Group in embattled Vietnam. He recalled the tediousness of the negotiations that preceded the signing of the Declaration that "truly taxed the goodwill, the imagination, the patience and understanding of the five participating Ministers." That ASEAN was established at all in spite of these difficulties, he said, meant that its foundations had been solidly laid. And he impressed it on the audience of diplomats, officials and media people who had witnessed the signing ceremony that a great sense of urgency had prompted the Ministers to go through all that trouble. He spoke darkly of the forces that were arrayed against the survival of the countries of Southeast Asia in those uncertain and critical times.

"The fragmented economies of Southeast Asia," he said, "(with) each country pursuing its own limited objectives and dissipating its meager resources in the overlapping or even conflicting endeavors of sister states carry the seeds of weakness in their incapacity for growth and their self-perpetuating dependence on the advanced, industrial nations. ASEAN, therefore, could marshal the still untapped potentials of this rich region through more substantial united action."

When it was his turn to speak, Adam Malik, Presidium Minister for Political Affairs and Minister for Foreign Affairs of Indonesia, recalled that about a year before, in Bangkok, at the conclusion of the peace talks between Indonesia and Malaysia, he had explored the idea of an organization such as ASEAN with his Malaysian and Thai counterparts. One of the "angry young men" in his country's struggle for independence two decades earlier, Adam Malik was then fifty years old and one of a Presidium of five led by then General Soeharto that was steering Indonesia from the verge of economic and political chaos. He was the Presidium's point man in Indonesia's efforts to mend fences with its neighbors in the wake of an unfortunate policy of confrontation. During the past year, he said, the Ministers had all worked together toward the realization of the ASEAN idea, "making haste slowly, in order to build a new association for regional cooperation."

Adam Malik went on to describe Indonesia's vision of a Southeast Asia developing into "a region which can stand on its own feet, strong enough to defend itself against any negative influence from outside the region." Such a vision, he stressed, was not wishful thinking, if the countries of the region effectively cooperated with each other, considering their combined natural resources and manpower. He referred to differences of outlook among the member countries, but those differences, he said, would be overcome through a maximum of goodwill and understanding, faith and realism. Hard work, patience and perseverance, he added, would also be necessary.

The countries of Southeast Asia should also be willing to take responsibility for whatever happens to them, according to Tun Abdul Razak, the Deputy Prime Minister of Malaysia, who spoke next. In his speech, he conjured a vision of an ASEAN that would include all the countries of Southeast Asia. Tun Abdul Razak was then concurrently his country's Minister of Defence and Minister of National Development. It was a time when national survival was the overriding thrust of Malaysia's relations with other nations and so as Minister of Defence, he was in charge of his country's foreign affairs. He stressed that the countries of the region should recognize that unless they assumed their common responsibility to shape their own destiny and to prevent external intervention and interference, Southeast Asia would remain fraught with danger and tension. And unless they took decisive and collective action to prevent the eruption of intra-regional conflicts, the nations of Southeast Asia would remain susceptible to manipulation, one against another.

"We the nations and peoples of Southeast Asia," Tun Abdul Razak said, "must get together and form by ourselves a new perspective and a new framework for our region. It is important that individually and jointly we should create a deep awareness that we cannot survive for long as independent but isolated peoples unless we also think and act together and unless we prove by deeds that we belong to a family of Southeast Asian nations bound together by ties of friendship and goodwill and imbued with our own ideals and aspirations and determined to shape our own destiny". He added that, "with the establishment of ASEAN, we have taken a firm and a bold step on that road".

For his part, S. Rajaratnam, a former Minister of Culture of multicultural Singapore who, at that time, served as its first foreign minister, noted that two decades of nationalist fervor had not fulfilled the expectations of the people of Southeast Asia for better living standards. If ASEAN would succeed, he said, then its members would have to marry national thinking with regional thinking.

"We must now think at two levels," Rajaratnam said. "We must think not only of our national interests but posit them against regional interests: that is a new way of thinking about our problems. And these are two different things and sometimes they can conflict. Secondly, we must also accept the fact, if we are really serious about it, that regional existence means painful adjustments to those practices and thinking in our respective countries. We must make these painful and difficult adjustments. If we are not going to do that, then regionalism remains a utopia."

S. Rajaratnam expressed the fear, however, that ASEAN would be misunderstood. "We are not against anything", he said, "not against anybody". And here he used a term that would have an ominous ring even today: balkanization. In Southeast Asia, as in Europe and any part of the world, he said, outside powers had a vested interest in the balkanization of the region. "We want to ensure," he said, "a stable Southeast Asia, not a balkanized Southeast Asia. And those countries who are interested, genuinely interested, in the stability of Southeast Asia, the prosperity of Southeast Asia, and better economic and social conditions, will welcome small countries getting together to pool their collective resources and their collective wisdom to contribute to the peace of the world."

The goal of ASEAN, then, is to create, not to destroy. This, the Foreign Minister of Thailand, Thanat Khoman, stressed when it was his turn to speak. At a time when the Vietnam conflict was raging and American forces seemed forever entrenched in Indochina, he had foreseen their eventual withdrawal from the area and had accordingly applied himself to adjusting Thailand's foreign policy to a reality that would only become apparent more than half a decade later. He must have had that in mind when, on that occasion, he said that the countries of Southeast Asia had no choice but to adjust to the exigencies of the time, to move toward closer cooperation and even integration. Elaborating on ASEAN objectives, he spoke of "building a new society that will be responsive to the needs of our time and efficiently equipped to bring about, for the enjoyment and the material as well as spiritual advancement of our peoples, conditions of stability and progress. Particularly what millions of men and women in our part of the world want is to erase the old and obsolete concept of domination and subjection of the past and replace it with the new spirit of give and take, of equality and partnership. More than anything else, they want to be master of their own house and to enjoy the inherent right to decide their own destiny."

While the nations of Southeast Asia prevent attempts to deprive them of their freedom and sovereignty, he said, they must first free themselves from the material impediments of ignorance, disease and hunger. Each of these nations cannot accomplish that alone, but by joining together and cooperating with those who have the same aspirations, these objectives become easier to attain. Then Thanat Khoman concluded: "What we have decided today is only a small beginning of what we hope will be a long and continuous sequence of accomplishments of which we ourselves, those who will join us later and the generations to come, can be proud. Let it be for Southeast Asia, a potentially rich region, rich in history, in spiritual as well as material resources and indeed for the whole ancient continent of Asia, the light of happiness and well-being that will shine over the uncounted millions of our struggling peoples."

The Foreign Minister of Thailand closed the inaugural session of the Association of Southeast Asian Nations by presenting each of his colleagues with a memento. Inscribed on the memento presented to the Foreign Minister of Indonesia, was the citation, "In recognition of services rendered by His Excellency Adam Malik to the ASEAN organization, the name of which was suggested by him."

And that was how ASEAN was conceived, given a name, and born. It had been barely 14 months since Thanat Khoman brought up the ASEAN idea in his conversations with his Malaysian and Indonesian colleagues. In about three more weeks, Indonesia would fully restore diplomatic relations with Malaysia, and soon after that with Singapore. That was by no means the end to intra-ASEAN disputes, for soon the Philippines and Malaysia would have a falling out on the issue of sovereignty over Sabah. Many disputes between ASEAN countries persist to this day. But all Member Countries are deeply committed to resolving their differences through peaceful means and in the spirit of mutual accommodation. Every dispute would have its proper season but it would not be allowed to get in the way of the task at hand. And at that time, the essential task was to lay the framework of regional dialogue and cooperation.

The two-page Bangkok Declaration not only contains the rationale for the establishment of ASEAN and its specific objectives. It represents the organization's modus operandi of building on small steps, voluntary, and informal arrangements toward more binding and institutionalized agreements. All the founding member states and the newer members have stood fast to the spirit of the Bangkok Declaration. Over the years, ASEAN has progressively entered into several formal and legally binding instruments, such as the 1976 Treaty of Amity and Cooperation in Southeast Asia and the 1995 Treaty on the Southeast Asia Nuclear Weapon-Free Zone.

Against the backdrop of conflict in the then Indochina, the Founding Fathers had the foresight of building a community of and for all Southeast Asian states. Thus the Bangkok Declaration promulgated that "the Association is open for participation to all States in the Southeast Asian region subscribing to the aforementioned aims, principles and purposes." ASEAN's inclusive outlook has paved the way for community-building not only in Southeast Asia, but also in the broader Asia-Pacific region where several other intergovernmental organizations now co-exist.

The original ASEAN logo presented five brown sheaves of rice stalks, one for each founding member. Beneath the sheaves is the legend "ASEAN" in blue. These are set on a field of yellow encircled by a blue border. Brown stands for strength and stability, yellow for prosperity and blue for the spirit of cordiality in which ASEAN affairs are conducted. When ASEAN celebrated its 30th Anniversary in 1997, the sheaves on the logo had increased to ten – representing all ten countries of Southeast Asia and reflecting the colors of the flags of all of them. In a very real sense, ASEAN and Southeast Asia would then be one and the same, just as the Founding Fathers had envisioned.

This article is based on the first chapter of ASEAN at 30, a publication of the Association of Southeast Asian Nations in commemoration of its 30th Anniversary on August 8, 1997, written by Jamil Maidan Flores and Jun Abad.

Further readings in ASEAN history:

Thanat Khoman, "ASEAN Conception and Evolution", in the ASEAN Reader, Institute of Southeast Asian Studies, Singapore, 1992.

S. Rajaratnam, "ASEAN: The Way Ahead", in The ASEAN Reader, Institute of Southeast Asian Studies, Singapore, 1992.

INDEX

For EU product safety concerns, contact us at Calle de José Abascal, 56–1°, 28003 Madrid, Spain or eugpsr@cambridge.org.

www.ingramcontent.com/pod-product-compliance
Lightning Source LLC
LaVergne TN
LVHW052109210926
848482LV00024B/387
* 9 7 8 1 3 1 6 6 0 4 3 1 1 *